Who's In Charge Here?

The Complex Relationship Between Ministry and Authority

A Report by the Commission on Appraisal

June 2013

Unitarian Universalist Association of Congregations
Boston

Boston, Massachusetts

Printed in the United States

Cover and text design by Suzanne Morgan

print ISBN: 978-1-55896-708-3
eBook ISBN: 978-1-55896-709-0

6 5 4 3 2 1
15 14 13

We gratefully acknowledge permission to reprint "Take courage friends . . ." by Wayne Arnason.

Library of Congress Cataloging-in-Publication Data
Unitarian Universalist Commission on Appraisal.
  Who's in charge here? : the complex relationship between ministry and authority : a report / by the Commission on Appraisal, Unitarian Universalist Association.
    pages cm
  "June 2013."
  Includes bibliographical references.
  ISBN 978-1-55896-708-3 (pbk. : alk. paper)—ISBN 978-1-55896-709-0 (ebook)
1. Authority—Religious aspects—Unitarian Universalist churches. 2. Church work—Unitarian Universalist churches. 3. Pastoral theology—Unitarian Universalist churches. 4. Unitarian Universalist churches—Doctrines. I. Title.
  BX9850.U56 2013
  262'.09132—dc23
                                2013005378

Who's In Charge Here?

Contents

This report is dedicated with love
to our colleague Don Mohr.

Preface and Acknowledgments

This book has been prepared by the Commission on Appraisal of the Unitarian Universalist Association of Congregations (UUA). This is the thirteenth report of the Commission since its inauguration under the Bylaws of the UUA in 1961. The Commission consists of nine members; three are elected by the General Assembly every other year for six-year terms. The Commission is charged with reviewing any function or activity of the UUA that it believes would benefit from independent review and with reporting on its review to the General Assembly at least once every four years.

Writing a report such as this is a complex task that requires the help of many people. We express our deep appreciation to the Publications Office of the UUA and especially to our editor, Marshall Hawkins, who shepherded this project through the publication process.

We also extend our gratitude to the following people who met with us for individual interviews, sharing their unique perspectives and wisdom with us: Joy Atkinson, Steve Beckner, Karen Brammer, Howard Dana, Janne Eller-Isaacs, Ian Evison, Lisa Friedman, Doug Gallagher, Clyde Grubbs, Bill Hamilton-Holway, James Hobart, Deborah Holder, Keith Kron, Sarah Lammert, Harlan Limpert, Bob Miess, Beth Miller, Jake Morrill, Lisa Presley, Christine Robinson, Don Southworth, and John Weston. We also thank everyone who contributed their wisdom in our online discussions with interim ministers and ministerial settlement representatives.

We deeply appreciate all those Unitarian Universalists who participated in our focus groups. Their stories and perspectives are the heart of this report, and we are so grateful to have been entrusted with their words. Focus group participants were assured that they would be anonymous in this report and are referred to throughout with pseudonyms.

This report has multiple authors. Each of the Commissioners wrote specific sections, and all commented on and improved on each other's work. We take joint responsibility for the endeavor. The current Commissioners appreciate the work of the former Commissioners who contributed to the early stages of the report but who were no longer serving by the time of publication: Barbara Child, Jacqui C. Williams, Michael Ohlrogge, and Mitra Rahnema. Finally, we extend our appreciation and gratitude to former Commissioner Don Mohr, who passed away before the report could be finished. We dedicate this work to him. The Commission invites comments on this report, and on other matters of concern to the UUA. Comments or inquiries may be addressed to: coa@uua.org.

Rev. Erica Baron, Rutland, Vermont

Rev. John Cullinan, Los Alamos, New Mexico

Megan Dowdell, Oakland, California

Peter Fontneau, Springfield, Virginia

Rev. Lynne Garner, Brunswick, Georgia

Bev Harrison, Campbell, California, and Foster, Rhode Island

Rev. Dr. Nana' Kratochvil, Muskegon, Michigan

About the Current Commissioners

Erica Baron brings to this work a passion for the practice of ministry and for the place of covenants in our congregations. She is proud to have been the project manager for this report and expresses her deep gratitude to the other Commissioners, both those currently on the Commission and those who have left, for coming with her on this journey. While writing this report, she has been the minister of the Unitarian Universalist Church of Rutland and the Unitarian Universalist Fellowship of Bennington, both in Vermont.

John Cullinan has been inspired by the work of the Commission for many years and is honored to be able to contribute to his chosen faith by continuing its work. He is passionate about finding new avenues through which ministry and authority can be shared within the congregation. While John was somewhat intimidated by joining this effort midstream, his fellow Commissioners made the transition easy and he is grateful for their presence and hard work. John serves as minister of the Unitarian Church of Los Alamos, New Mexico.

Megan Dowdell, who chaired the Commission during the last two years, brings to this report a deep concern about the intersection of religious life and struggles for collective liberation and health. She is grateful for her relationships with current and past Commissioners and for the opportunity to have served the UUA through volunteer service for the past ten years. She is currently a candidate for UU ministry and a doctoral student in medical sociology at the University of California, San Francisco, where she focuses on bioethics and racial disparities in health. She also teaches at Starr King School for the Ministry in Berkeley, California, as an adjunct professor.

Pete Fontneau has been inspired by the friends with whom he served on the Commission over the last six years, sharing discussions, surveying and reviewing data, and drafting text. He applied his lay leadership experience at Accotink Unitarian Universalist Church in Burke, Virginia, and his ongoing seminary training to forging language for this report. He matured as a church member, as a leader, and as a religious person. He was humbled by the trust placed in him and thanks all those with whom he interacted during this work.

Lynne Garner joined the Commission midway through this project and is grateful to her fellow Commissioners for choosing such an important and interesting topic to study. She has found the process of putting this report together both stimulating and challenging. A Unitarian Universalist from childhood, she is honored to follow in the footsteps of past Commissioners, whose previous reports have helped shape her ministry. She serves as minister to the Unitarian Universalists of Coastal Georgia in Brunswick, Georgia.

Bev Harrison brings a lay perspective based on leadership in several congregations on both the east and west coasts. She is currently a member at Westminster Unitarian Church in East Greenwich, Rhode Island, and First Unitarian Church of San Jose, California. She is grateful for the opportunity to share in the work of the Commission and thanks the minister who first suggested that she serve.

Nana' Kratochvil cares deeply about congregational health and has served as a minister and in larger arenas to grow churches and increase membership. She believes that healthy congregations help develop healthy cultures in which to live. She is now retired and is ready to look for a community with such a church. She is minister emerita of Harbor Unitarian Universalist Congregation in Muskegon, Michigan, and consulting minister for the Unitarian Universalist Fellowship of Central Michigan. She has found serving with her fellow Commissioners to be a joy and a privilege.

A Note About Language

Language is organic and changeable, and so we have found it necessary to make some decisions about the ways we will refer to people and communities. We note here some of the usage we have chosen, along with our reasons.

LGBTQ: The acronym for this community changes and grows regularly. We have chosen this as an inclusive term born from the community itself. The acronym stands for Lesbian, Gay, Bisexual, Transgender/Genderqueer, Queer, and Questioning. When directly quoting others, we have used their language.

They/Their: We carefully considered which pronouns to use when referring to people whose gender is not easily labeled as male or female, and which to use when referring to a general categories of people. In both cases, we have decided to use the pronouns *they* and *their*. Such usage has been common in casual spoken English for quite some time, and has growing support as a way to refer to people without defining their gender.

Transgender/Genderqueer and Cisgender: In searching for terms to describe the transgender/genderqueer community, we found the words of Eric Anthony Grollman instructive and decided to adopt this usage. Grollman explains:

In the past few decades, especially these past ten years, transgender people have become increasingly visible as a part of the US population. The term "transgender" is generally used to refer to a person whose sex (i.e., anatomy, hormones, chromosomes) is inconsistent with their gender (i.e., sense of self, behavior, appearance). . . . But, not everyone whose gender and sex are incongruent want to change their sex to become the "opposite sex." People who identify as "genderqueer," a rather new term used mostly among young adults, experience this incongruence, but experience gender as neither woman nor man. . . . Genderqueer people challenge the idea of two genders (woman and man) and sexes (female and male); rather, they seek to blur such binaries. . . . Finally, the gender term that is least known about, but describes the vast majority of people in the world, is cisgender. "Cisgender" refers to people whose sex and gender are congruent by predominant cultural standards: women who have female bodies, men who have male bodies. This term was created to challenge . . . the privileging of such people in the term "gender" relative to the term "transgender." For example, in referring to "transmen" (female-to-male transgender men) and "men" (cismen), it may seem that transgender men are always a special type of "man," while men are, without question, "real men."[1]

Notes

1. Eric Anthony Grollman, October 5, 2012, "Transgender, Genderqueer, Cisgender . . . . What Do These Terms Mean?" *Kinsey Confidential: Sexual Health Information from the Kinsey Institute*, accessed January 24, 2013, www.kinseyconfidential.org/transgender-genderqueer-cisgender-terms.

An Introductory Case Study

The Commission on Appraisal's process for this report began with a year of topic selection and refinement. We solicited suggestions for a new topic through an online survey, and received roughly three hundred replies. In deciding among these suggestions, we looked for a topic that would allow us to dig deep and make significant contributions to Unitarian Universalism today. Ministry stood out as having the most promise, and we chose to include ministry as practiced by both lay members of our congregations and professional clergy. We recognized that many of the struggles and stresses around ministry in Unitarian Universalist congregations stem from issues of authority. Our topic thus became the complex relationship between ministry and authority.

We know that congregations are not the only places where people are living out Unitarian Universalism. Vital ministries take place outside the congregation, in settings such as hospitals, non-profit organizations, college campuses, prisons, and military bases. And there are many who identify as Unitarian Universalists who are not formal members of Unitarian Universalist congregations but who still live out UU principles and values, and who sometimes gather in other kinds of communities. For an in-depth discussion of these extra-congregational expressions of Unitarian Universalism, see the report *Congregations and Beyond* released in September 2012 by UUA President Peter Morales.

Who's In Charge Here?, however, focuses specifically on the relationship between ministry and authority within Unitarian Universalist

text continues on page 5

Composite Case Study 1

Profile

Congregation Name: Unitarian Universalist Fellowship of East Lyndon

Members: 83

City Population: 17,000

County Population: 30,000

Region: Midwest

Professional Staff: Part-time Minister (Rev. Donna Hitchens), quarter-time Office Administrator

The Situation

The congregation was founded as a fellowship in 1952. After a long period with no ministry, they hired a consulting minister in 1975. Since then, they have had periods of settled ministry, periods of interim ministry, and periods without professional ministry. The current minister has been serving there for three years and is generally well liked. There was a conflict about worship at the beginning of her ministry, which has calmed down, but some people are still angry about it.

The Minister

The minister discusses the congregation's history of shared ministry.

> *Rev. Hitchens*: The church has had a lot of conflict in the last ten years, [but] during their heyday, they had a very strong shared ministry structure and even a paid Shared Ministry Coordinator. So I think that they were kind of looking to get back to the idea of shared ministry. Which is really interesting to me, too, because how do you hold—and maybe this is getting ahead of the process, but I'm an extrovert and process out loud so—how do you hold shared ministry and [have] such a fantastic view of professional ministry and authority?

Interviewer: Turn your attention to professional clergy who minister to congregations. Where do you think they get the authority to do their ministry and to make decisions about how they will do it?

Rev. Hitchens: I mean, there's so many [factors]—your education, your experience. You know, what I wrote down was, "By what authority?" . . . and I started writing these down: congregation, education, experience, credentialing, you know, etc., etc. . . . and the only thing that I could come up with to kind of pull them all together is that it's affirmed by the congregation. All of these levels of authority are affirmed by the congregation. I can be called to be a minister, and I can be educated, and I can be credentialed, and I can be ordained . . . but the congregation affirms that. And there's something in that affirming process and that relationship.

Interviewer: And if that's missing, then the other ones count for little?

Rev. Hitchens: They do, but this is where my experience with the fellowships in the upper Midwest comes in. You got to have it, you know. I mean, I was doing ministry, whether the fellowship I was working with would grant me that or not [laughs]. . . . So, I wanted to have all of these different other levels, but it's the congregation that affirms.

One of the things that's come up in my mind as we were having this conversation is power: The relationship between authority and power. Because the congregation has the power to fire me . . . but there's a difference between power and authority, and so . . . what's the relationship between power and authority and how does that relate to ministry?

When asked about the relationship between power and authority in the congregation, the minister told the following story.

Rev. Hitchens: Before I was called to East Lyndon, both the interims shared that one woman in particular had been identified as some sort of—I don't know how this happened—but she had been identified, and it was documented, that she was the person who held the most power in the church. A lay person. And it didn't matter what position she held. It didn't matter if she has any position at all. Doesn't matter. She is the one who apparently has the most power in the church.

Interviewer: And is this true?

Rev. Hitchens: And it is . . . and so, I've kept her so close, making sure that she and I have a fabulous relationship. Because she does—she has the power to make or break my ministry.

Interviewer: In your congregational experience, to what extent do differences of opinion about ministry and authority contribute to congregational stresses and strains?

Rev. Hitchens: I came to our church after the previous minister was fired. And there was this kind of funny feeling and they had come out of the fellowship movement, so it was kind of interesting and I realized they needed a light hand. And it's surprising how long it has had to be a light hand in some places. I happened to be listening in the arts of ministry class where the professor said fellowships can really be fractious so be careful. So, I . . . (they are a really good group of people and I don't want to lose sight of that) so there was a time for the first year or so that they didn't know what to do with me in some ways. Oddly enough, normally actually it goes pretty smoothly. The one place where . . . differences of opinion about ministry and authority come up [as] stresses/strains . . . is on the Sunday Service Committee, because you are a person with the training and me being the person with the accountability, I have a tendency to want to do things my way or at least be handling the tiller on that one. So, where am I going with this is that the answer to your question is, "You bet." It causes the most stresses and strains in an area where I really have to exert some authority if I want a quality product that will bring people into the sanctuary where I am really accountable.

The Sunday Services Committee

Brad: First of all, from the other discussion, I would say that [having a] minister is not critical to ministry in church. There are those congregations that don't have a minister and everything you described about your congregation was . . . if you didn't have a minister, it would go on. If you had a church administrator but not a minister, I bet your ministry would work really well. Now, that's not to say that, whoever the minister is, is not contributing and leading and giving you ideas and stuff, but it struck me that what you're talking about was a community that was making ministry and that you could change ministers. . . . But the minister itself was not a critical element of making ministry in the church, that was the first thing.

Cathy: I had a conversation yesterday in a social environment which we talked about church. Somebody was mentioning the fact that they came from a Christian church in which the minister made everything happen. . . . They defined the church in many ways, and that in our experience as Unitarians, that does not happen. I don't want to call the minister an employee of the congregation, but there is a sense in my mind in which the minister is kind of like an employee more than in a Christian church. Even though they are administering, they're not leading the ministry or defining ministry in some way. I think the group defines what the ministry is and the minister participates and matches that and leads that in some way but I don't think the minister defines that.

Julie: We've gone back and forth between having part-time ministers and not, and people that really wanted a minister, and people have disagreed about whether they want a full-time or half-time [minister], but it was wanting that focal person, that leader, that for us is the message of Unitarian Universalism that's inspirational. The reason you go to church on Sunday is to hear this guy and everything else is kind of scattered around, it just seems to me that he's the focal point. And also he sees people on an individual basis. It's not therapy but it's close to [it] . . . and nobody else has that function.

Bob: When you asked about ministering . . . I didn't think of how the congregation as a whole minister[s], I was thinking of how the minister minister[s] . . . I thought of the individual. . . . [Ministers] deal with individuals in terms of issues that they had and health issues, so they're in jail or whatever, I don't know. But [ministers] have that special something about them that says because they are a minister, reverend, or whatever, they had the special reason, something to connect to the individual to work with them, to help them in their time of need. And so in my mind, I was thinking of the more narrow idea of pastoring.

The Board

Linda (Board President): This is a little bit hard to explain; it might seem like I'm going all over the map but I'll try not to. When we were between ministers, [it] came up at an annual congregational meeting whether or not we wanted or did not want to bring in an interim minister. And there was a group of people that said no, that we could save the money and this would be a wonderful opportunity for lay leadership and . . . they presented the case for not bringing in a minister during that time of search.

One of the problems with that is that this self-appointed group kind of wanted to run the show. They saw themselves as the leaders and the authority figures and they wanted to step up to the point. Part of the congregation said, "No, we really need that ministry there." And I don't say this unkindly, but nevertheless, I think you know what I mean—we keep this [type of] people kind of at bay. Yes, they have talents and they want to step up to the plate and they want to . . . do their part but that's not always appreciated or needed or wanted. So it was important at that time to bring in a minister to . . . be that authority figure that would sort of neutralize all those feelings about who is the authority figure.

Bruce: We've had ministers who we have not respected and we had a lot of problems with and therefore they are not an authority figure. They lost ground with us; things went bad and it was not a good situation. And so using the term "authority figure" for that kind of minister that did not have a lot of respect from congregants. You couldn't even use the word "authority figure." And then we've had other ministers who've been greatly respected and have had kind of a hands-off approach and they're more of an authority figure, so it's kind of the person itself and how congregants feel about that person. They don't take authority, we give them the authority or not.

Mary: The hard question for us is who owns the Sunday service? The authority of the pulpit is a question that arose because we had a new minister. The congregation was accustomed to congregational response and the minister didn't want it. We on the Worship Committee heard that the minister has the choice of how to run the worship service. Okay. I've been a member of this committee for years. The Worship Committee was getting a lot of conversation from congregation members who wanted it. The chair really got it. It caused conflict for a long time. What this brought up for me was [the question of] where was the listening of that minister? Why wasn't there more of her asking why they wanted congregational response: "Let's talk about congregational response. Let me hear what you think." A whole group who wanted congregational response siphoned themselves out of Sunday services, came and had their own discussion group on Sunday morning. They clung together. [There were other] people who were willing to cooperate and move on. I have loyalties in both camps. I ended up listening compassionately to people. I said part of my job was to help the minister. It was very difficult [and] brought up a lot of issues. How much integrity does this minister really have? If this minister is a caring person, doesn't she want to know? Why didn't she ask, "Why haven't you given this up in three years of my ministry?" There's a lot there for me.

congregations. This relationship in UU contexts other than congregations might be fruitful ground for examination in the future.

As we listened to the stories and experiences of Unitarian Universalists, we found that there is a great deal of tension around issues of authority in congregations. Some of this is the result of abuses of power or clearly inappropriate behavior. But more often, there is no clear right and wrong; instead there are important values in tension.

The Commission came to the conclusion that our values are foundational to our understanding of authority issues. As a Commission, we value quality worship. We believe that allowing leaders to have authority in the areas for which they are accountable is important. We also value shared ministry and the role of lay leadership in directing the ministry of a congregation. We believe that it is important for ministers to be able to exercise authority, just as it is important for lay leadership to be able to exercise authority. Finally, we believe it is important for all members of a congregation to have a voice in the direction and ministry of the congregation.

We believe that it is important for ministers to be able to exercise authority, just as it is important for lay leadership to be able to exercise authority.

However, in practice there is often a perception of tension between the exercise of ministerial authority and the exercise of lay authority. Our research has also found tension between having structures that are clearly defined and the need for flexibility, between honoring tradition and adapting to new conditions, and between the value of individualism and the value of community. These tensions can cause very real pain, but they are also the crucible which gives rise to new and dynamic forms of ministry.

The common struggles around authority in Unitarian Universalism intersect with the systems of power and privilege in our congregations and in society. In the conversations that formed this case study, we were struck by the members' desire for a minister who can neutralize tensions around authority, and by the sense that the right kind of minister has a hands-off approach. We heard similar conversations elsewhere.

We found that *neutral* is often code for *white* and *male* and we wonder whether there is an implicit understanding about who will be given authority (someone neutral), and who will not (someone who holds an identity that challenges members of the congregation). A minister's identities—including gender, race, and age—can affect the perception of whether the minister has a "hands-off" approach or is more aggressive. For example, the same behavior may be read as assertive by a white man but aggressive by a woman of color. So the perception of the minister's use of authority and the acceptance of that authority by the congregation are affected by the minister's identities, and by the congregation's perception of those identities.

The cultural standard of a white, straight, male minister is still in play, though this describes a shrinking minority of actual Unitarian Universalist ministers. The extent to which a given minister varies from this standard impacts the ways congregations and colleagues grant and withhold authority from that minister. This means that our struggles around authority and ministry fall most heavily on those furthest from the center of power and privilege in our national and Unitarian Universalist cultures.

Unitarian Universalists seek to create vibrant life-giving congregations which contribute to the personal and spiritual growth of their members and serve the spirit of liberation in the world. We aim to build congregations grounded in strong and vital covenants. As James Luther Adams said in a presentation in 1975, we seek to be congregations which call individuals into "a caring, trusting fellowship, that protects and nourishes their integrity and spiritual freedom. Its goal is the prophethood and priesthood of all believers— the one for the liberty of prophesying, the other for the ministry of healing."[1]

In order to do this, as Unitarian Universalists we need to become more skilled at navigating the tensions around ministry and authority in our congregations. *We need to be more attentive to bringing the margins into the center, and creating structures and systems which serve liberation rather than oppression.* We need to heal the pain caused by abuses of power in the past and work to prevent such abuses in the present and future. We need to revitalize our commitment to our covenants and missions, and to the spiritual resources which keep them strong and vital. We need to learn again how to trust one another and walk together in the work of ministry. We need a revitalized understanding of and commitment to shared ministry.

In the chapters ahead, after a description of our research methodology, the Commission looks at the historical and social contexts that contribute to our congregations' struggles with ministry and authority. We then consider what we mean by "ministry," followed by what we mean by "authority." We consider who does and does not have authority in UU congregations, and look in detail at the conflicts which arise in congregations around ministry and authority. Finally, we consider ways to respond which will move us back toward our aspirations and principles.

We invite you on this journey with words from Rev. Wayne Arnason:

Take courage friends.
The way is often hard, the path is never clear,
And the stakes are very high.
Take courage.
For deep down, there is another truth:
You are not alone.

Notes

1. James Luther Adams, "The Church That Is Free," in *The Prophethood of All Believers*, George K. Beach, ed. (Boston: Beacon Press, 1986), 313.

Our Research Methodology

Issues of authority within Unitarian Universalist congregations are complex. We offer here a picture of the ways authority functions to help or to hinder congregations and offer some possible responses for the times when systems of authority are not working well.

This report is the result of a three-pronged research approach. Our three major methods included consulting existing resources, conducting focus groups, and examining case studies. Within these methodologies, several different lenses were used in the interpretation and analysis of the information collected.

Existing Resources

When beginning any new study, it is important to know about other works that have addressed the topic. First, we looked for published books and articles within Unitarian Universalism and in religious publications more broadly that addressed issues of ministry, authority, clergy authority, lay ministry, shared ministry, power struggles, authority within systems theory, and other related topics. While we found many resources that informed our thinking, we did not find any text that addressed all of our research questions or that fully addressed the unique Unitarian Universalist approaches and struggles with authority. An annotated list of the most helpful resources can be found at the end of this book.

We also consulted those with expertise on questions of ministry and authority. This included conducting interviews with associational leaders and launching online forums to engage in specific topics with interim ministers and ministerial settlement representatives.

Focus Groups

We designed a collection of focus groups to explore our research questions in more detail and asked each group the same set of questions:

1. What is your name? What congregation are you from? How long have you been there? What drew you there?

2. We call some, but not all, things that happen in congregations *ministry*. What goes on in your congregation that you would call *ministry*? Who does these things? What goes on in the congregation that you consider not to be part of the ministry?

3a. Turn your attention now to professional clergy who minister to congregations. Where do you think they get the authority to do their ministry and to make decisions about how they will do it?

3b. Now turn your attention to the laypeople in congregations. What gives them the authority to make decisions that affect ministry in their congregations, especially the ministry carried out by professional clergy?

4a. In your congregational experience, to what extent do differences of opinion about ministry and authority contribute to congregational stresses and strains?

4b. What ideas do you have about how to overcome stresses and strains due to differences of opinion about ministry and authority?"

5. Based on your congregational experience, what else would you like the Commission to investigate and think about as we pursue our study of the relationship between ministry and authority?

A discussion guide for use in congregations, based on the guide used by moderators of the focus groups can be found on page 81.

Each focus group consisted of 6–12 people who shared certain characteristics related to our questions. Groups were moderated either by a member of the Commission or by a volunteer moderator using materials designed by the Commission. Each group was recorded and Commissioners created a transcript of the conversation.

Focus groups were organized in two ways. One set of groups included people with various roles or identities within the congregation, including parish ministers, community ministers, religious educators (paid and volunteer), Board members, committee chairs, musicians, members of committees on ministry, youth and young adults, and youth and young adults of color.

The other set of groups was designed to provide insight into the effects of personal identity on ministerial authority and was therefore organized by the self-defined identities of ministers, including male, female, transgender/genderqueer, and people of color. We also had a group of ministers in co-ministry situations.

We conducted 25 focus groups, in which 186 Unitarian Universalists participated. We also asked two of the focus group questions of attendees at our General Assembly hearing in 2011; we heard from another 24 people there.

Fifteen of these groups took place during two day-long gatherings held in conjunction with Commission meetings in Bloomington, Indiana, and Albany, New York. We made sure the rest of our groups were held around the country, with each of the five regions of the UUA represented multiple times. Some of the identity-based groups took place at General Assembly, which provided the best opportunity to gather enough people for a group.

As focus group participants shared their stories and perspectives, themes and patterns began to emerge. Patterns were sometimes identified in a linear fashion by noting the recurrence of certain words, phrases, and ideas. However, we also used several more intuitive exercises to find patterns and themes. We moved back and forth between the specifics of a particular conversation and the larger emerging patterns. Through this process, we began to draw conclusions about the ways many Unitarian Universalist congregations function around authority and noted places where the various social locations of participants created different experiences of authority in our congregations.

Using pseudonyms, we quote focus group participants throughout this report.

Case Studies

We decided early in the process that after using focus groups to look at *parts* of congregations, we wanted a way to look at the whole system. This is what led us to use case studies, which proved to be the most challenging part of the entire project. We planned to visit three or so congregations to do an in-depth study of issues of ministry and authority, allowing each congregation to choose whether it wished to be anonymous in our final report. However, after approaching a number of congregations, we could find no congregation willing to let us come do this kind of research. Congregations were unwilling even to talk about one pre-selected, resolved conflict. We considered this to be a significant indication of the sensitivity and importance of this topic.

As a result, we decided instead to create composite case studies for analysis using the focus group data from the two regional day-long focus group gatherings. For these meetings, congregations typically sent multiple representatives who participated in different focus groups. We noticed in the focus group transcripts that often the same story was shared from a variety of different viewpoints. For example, the minister of a congregation might be in one focus group while the Board president was in another, and the chair of the Religious Education Committee was in still another. It was therefore possible to reconstruct a composite view.

The Commission's project manager created two composite case studies using the transcripts from the two gatherings. The details were changed enough to disguise the people and congregations involved, but these case studies did arise out of conversations with Unitarian Universalists about their congregations. The complete case studies can be found on pages 2 and 42.

Lenses

In order to illuminate issues of power, privilege, and oppression woven into questions of ministry and authority, we analyzed our case studies through a series of lenses, inspired by black feminist and liberationist studies of congregational life. This approach was based largely on the work of Traci C. West.[1]

As a Commission, we rejected the idea that nine individuals could or should produce an objective Truth with a capital T on issues of authority and ministry in Unitarian Universalism. In our search for meaning in the stories we heard, we attempted to bring our individual and collective faith values to the analysis in an embodied way. We routinely asked ourselves, "Who are we and what do we value?"

In this process, we also sought to include our own engagement with cultural diversity to lead us through a process of developing intercultural competence. We spoke with Nehrwr Abdul-Wahid of One Ummah Consulting, an organizational consulting group which focuses on issues of intercultural competence and sensitivity. We then used the Intercultural Development Inventory® to look at our functioning as a Commission and as individuals in order to continue developing our intercultural competence.[2]

As a commission, we rejected the idea that nine individuals could or should produce an objective Truth with a capital T on issues of authority and ministry in Unitarian Universalism. In our search for meaning in the stories we heard, we attempted to bring our individual and collective faith values to the analysis in an embodied way.

In defining the problems our participants identified as central to the relationship between ministry and authority, we opened ourselves to being led by the voices of those holding marginalized identities. We hoped to bring their experiences to the center of our report, rather than simply extending a dominant or traditional view of authority to include oppressed groups. This process challenged us to engage difference with curiosity and brought us to a deeper understanding of the systems and institutions at work in conflicts around authority and ministry, as well as potential responses to these problems.

As part of our commitment to putting our understandings in an embodied context rather than assuming a universal lens, we turn first to a discussion of the historical and theological context which gave rise to the present experiences of authority and ministry in Unitarian Universalist congregations.

Notes

1. Traci C. West, *Disruptive Christian Ethics: When Racism and Women's Lives Matter* (Louisville, KY: Westminster John Knox Press, 2006).
2. The Intercultural Development Inventory is a registered trademark of IDI, LLC in the United States and other countries.

Historical and Cultural Context

The context of conflicts over ministry and authority must be described through several historical perspectives. First we turn to a discussion of the authority of professional clergy and lay members of our congregations as it has changed over time. Then we explore the experiences of particular communities in ministry, including people of color, women, and LGBTQ people. As part of a faith tradition that is rooted in the context of the United States, our congregations feel the effects of the shifts in US culture over time.

Professional Ministry

Several key documents, movements, and moments of public controversy have shaped the authority of the professional minister: the Cambridge Platform, the humanist movement, movements to abolish slavery, the debate over the role of church in World War I, the civil rights movement, and decline of clergy authority in the late twentieth and early twenty-first centuries.

The Cambridge Platform of 1648 set up a view of clergy as valued leaders whose authority came both from education and vocation, but the Platform also defined congregational authority to hire and fire a minister. It was a statement of doctrine and polity adopted by a synod of Congregational ministers from Massachusetts and Connecticut. The Platform defines roles for "preachers and teachers," often the same person in a given congrega-

As part of a faith tradition that is rooted in the context of the United States, our congregations feel the effects of the shifts in US culture over time.

tion, who are called from among the people by election and serve to "attend chiefly to the ministry of the Word." These preachers and teachers were ordained to the ministry of the congregation by the congregation, who could also remove them in the case of "manifest unworthiness and delinquency." Along with its assertions on the right of the congregation to choose and, if necessary, to fire the clergy, the Platform also stressed the congregation's obligation to "most willingly submit to their ministry in the Lord."[1]

From this colonial era up until the onset of the twentieth century, this view of professional clergy remained intact. Early in the twentieth century, however, both Universalism and Unitarianism were shaped by the humanist movement, particularly in the Western Unitarian Conference. In congregations where traditional theological authority was open for debate or even scorned, the stage was set for other challenges of authority, including that of the ordained clergy. Once ministers were no longer seen as being called by God and ordained with God's blessing, the grounding for the authority of the minister lost some of its former justification.

Moments of public controversy have provided a context for congregations to challenge the authority of their ministers, especially if the minister publicly took an unpopular stand. In the years leading up to the Civil War, Unitarians were often divided on the issue of the abolition of slavery. In William Ellery Channing's congregation, for example, a significant percentage of the membership owned businesses that depended heavily on Southern slave labor, and so Channing found it difficult to speak out publicly in favor of abolition without jeopardizing his position in the pulpit. When at last he did, he found his role as a religious authority challenged by those members who were invested in the slave trade, and he was frequently shunned in public.[2] In contrast, his friend Theodore Parker led a thriving congregation in the same city while being an ardent and vocal abolitionist.[3]

During World War I, public controversy called into question the role of professional clergy authority. At the 1917 Unitarian General Conference, conference moderator and former US President William Howard Taft declared, "It is the duty of our church to preach the righteousness of the war and the necessity for our winning it in the interest of the peace of the world."[4]

The Board of the American Unitarian Association (AUA) also voted to deny financial aid to any church whose minister did not support the war. Pacifist minister John Haynes Holmes publicly confronted Taft, and afterward the AUA all but withdrew Holmes's Unitarian fellowship over the issue of the war. Eventually, the AUA apologized and welcomed Holmes and his church back into fellowship.

In the controversies over abolition and war, there was evident tension between religious principle and popular national sentiment, and the granting or revocation of authority to ministers often involved a dance along the razor's edge between these two competing forces.

Unitarian Universalists would see these tensions play out again in the civil rights era. Thousands of clergy and lay members joined in the marches and protests of the early days of that movement, but as civil rights legislation became reality, many of those same people were unwilling or unable to engage in the more radical action needed to move civil rights from legal charter to reality. What Jean Ott calls the "white controversy over black empowerment," described in more detail later in this chapter, not only tore the UUA apart, but also presented challenges to clergy authority depending on the attitudes of their respective congregations.[5]

In the past few decades the status, and with that the authority, of professional clergy in the United States has suffered a decline. Sexual misconduct, financial fraud, and other public scandals have dimmed the view of clergy in the eyes of the American public. A general lack of trust of organized religion along with the rise of the "spiritual but not religious" have further diminished that regard.

Lay Ministry

Events and documents throughout our Unitarian, Universalist, and Unitarian Universalist histories have also influenced the authority of lay ministry, including its relationship to professional ministry. The Cambridge Platform not only defined certain roles for pastors and teachers, it also called for a group of "called ruling elders" to "attend especially unto rule." These elders shared authority in the congregations with pastors and teachers, "because ruling and governing is common to these with the other."[6] From the Platform and from the traditions of the Reformation, lay members of our congregations have always contributed to the ministry and have always enjoyed a certain degree of authority within Unitarian, Universalist, and Unitarian Universalist congregations.

Once Ralph Waldo Emerson, in the nineteenth century, relocated the center of religious authority from the realm of hierarchy to individual experience, that sense of personal authority increased. Although the rise of the Transcendentalist movement was looked down on in early Unitarianism, it lives on today in the central liberal religious tenet of the "free and responsible search for truth and meaning."

John Dietrich and Curtis Reese were the first Unitarians to identify themselves as humanists. Reese considered humanism a "religion of democracy." In 1916, he preached that while the theocratic worldview is autocratic, the humanistic worldview is democratic. For Dietrich, humanism provided followers with "a firm and confident reliance upon themselves." Such views tended to equalize the playing field in congregations. This theology of democracy and self-reliance minimized the hierarchy historically

Lay members of our congregations have always contributed to the ministry and have always enjoyed authority within Unitarian, Universalist, and Unitarian Universalist congregations.

associated with congregational life, and greatly diminished the authority formerly granted to the minister. The minister no longer had a closer connection to the divine than anyone else, and therefore, could not claim a higher authority than the laity.[7]

Beginning in the 1930s, Sophia Lyon Fahs transformed the Unitarian children's religious education curriculum into one centered on experience, especially in nature, in order to capitalize on children's natural sense of wonder. Fahs was the author, co-author, and editor of many volumes in *The New Beacon Series*, which was also used by some other denominations. In 1959, at the age of 82, her life work was honored when she was ordained into the Unitarian ministry in Bethesda, Maryland, by the church that had the nation's largest religious education program of the time.[8]

The Fellowship Movement, a program of intentional lay-led church planting that took place in the 1950s and 1960s, brought with it a spirit of independence of the laity that is still prominent within the surviving congregations, even those that have prospered and later called ministers. This self-determination among the laity has made some congregations prosper, but has also led to conflict with ministers, whose authority has not always been recognized or accepted. Many members came into fellowships ignorant of Unitarianism's history and its connections to the longer history of its religious ancestors. This sense of isolation and independent genesis often led to a general sense of mistrust of denominational or indeed any external authority, and this pattern is still prevalent in these congregations to this day.[9]

The declining esteem for professional clergy in general today has resulted in a corresponding rise in trust in lay authority in many places around the country. The rise of the "spiritual but not religious" population points to a general rise in confidence in personal religious authority over clerical. Within institutional religion, especially Protestant Evangelical denominations, there is a professed mistrust of "trained" clergy, whose education is perceived as getting in the way of personal interpretation of scripture and confusing the individual's personal relationship with God. Most recently, the Pew Forum noted the rise in the number of individuals claiming to be unaffiliated with any religion or to have no religion at all; nearly 80 percent of them left the religion in which they were raised (of that number, 18 percent of Catholics and 25 percent of Protestants who now regard themselves as unaffiliated point to dissatisfaction with clergy as a reason for leaving).[10]

The idea of individual religious authority is now enshrined in our Principles and our membership is drawn to us because of that very liberty. As we'll come to see, tension and conflict often arise when multiple individual authorities attempt to build community together, in a culture that has come to mistrust institutional authority.

We next turn our attention to some examples of the differing impact our history and cultural context have had on people with marginalized identities who have sought ordination and have served in ministry in our congregations.

People of Color in UU Ministry

African Americans have sought ordination in the Unitarian, Universalist, and Unitarian Universalist movements since at least the mid-nineteenth century. One of the earliest to succeed was Joseph Fletcher Jordan, who was ordained to the Universalist ministry in 1889. Examples of those able to break down the barriers to ministry in the last few centuries are few and far between. They faced significant opposition from leaders within both the Unitarian and the Universalist movements.

For example, in 1935 Jeffrey Campbell graduated from seminary and was granted fellowship and ordained, yet the state superintendent objected to what he considered a waste of money in educating a "colored" minister.[11] In 1958, Rev. David H. Eaton was told by American Unitarian Association Vice President Dana Greeley, "I'd love to have you but we'll have trouble settling you."[12] These ministers' stories show a significant lack of the institutional support necessary to find and sustain positions in ministry.

After the passage of the Civil Rights Act, the UUA found itself unprepared for the next steps in racial justice and the more radical actions needed to make that justice a reality. The Unitarian Universalist community became divided over the best way to empower African-American laity and clergy in the "white controversy over black empowerment."

UU minister and historian Mark Morrison-Reed tells this story in his article "The Empowerment Tragedy." We enter his narrative at an Emergency Conference at the Biltmore Hotel in New York in October 1967:

> As rioting engulfed city after city, it became clear that legislation had not addressed African-American poverty or frustration . . . 37 of the 150 attendees were African Americans. They made up 25 percent of a gathering in a denomination of which they comprised only 1 percent, hailing from the urban churches in a faith community that was becoming more and more suburban.
>
> Soon after the conference began, thirty-three of the African Americans . . . withdrew from the planned agenda to hold their own meeting. Seminarian Thom Payne, an imposing presence, was posted at the door to shoo white interlopers away. This black caucus met through the evening and late into the night. As they talked, they tapped into the raw emotion hidden behind middle-class

reasonableness. They searched for an identity more authentic than the futile attempt to be carbon copies of white people. They saw white liberalism's emphasis on integration as a one-way street that elevated white and debased black. Civil rights had changed the law but had proven ineffective at remedying black poverty; liberal religion had failed to address the experience of blackness or to settle an African American in a major pulpit. The group called for a new agenda, and by the time they emerged, the Black Unitarian Universalist Caucus (BUUC) Steering Committee had been formed. They insisted that their agenda be voted up or down without debate, and that included a resolution that $1 million (12 percent of the UUA budget) be directed toward the black community over a period of four years. . . .

The conference sent shock waves through the UUA. Ben Scott . . . recalled, "It was also traumatic. I am not the only UU who was irreversibly shaped by it. Thousands were born again. They came to a better understanding of the whole world. . . . They came to a thrilling sense of the awesome potential of human society. In our little UU corner of the world, lifelong friendships crumbled, marriages dissolved, careers were ended . . . and congregations factionalized." Scott's words only hint at the intensity of the feelings. For many, what happened during the ensuing years would be nothing less than life-defining. . . .

The first National Conference of Black Unitarian Universalists gathered in Chicago in February 1968, with 207 attending. In May, a group of Afro- and Euro-Americans calling itself the Black and White Alternative, later changed to Black and White Action (BAWA), organized in New York City. On April 4, King was slain. In June, the General Assembly met in Cleveland. In the GA business meeting, the BAC funding proposal was placed on the agenda, and in an atmosphere of extraordinary emotional tension, the proponents of BAWA and the BAC competed for the support of the delegates. On the third day of the assembly, the delegates voted 836 to 327 to fund the BAC at $250,000 a year for four years. In the aftermath of King's death, what white person, given the guilt they felt, was going to vote against a resolution coming out of the BAC? The delegates also voted to give $50,000 to BAWA, over the protest of the BAC.

Following GA, the UUA board voted to give the BAC $250,000 for that year but not subsequent ones. It also learned that all its discretionary reserves had been depleted by the ambitious agenda and vision of President Greeley, then approaching the end of his term. The following spring, the administration recommended that the sum given to the BAC not be reduced. The Board supported that position as well as another, not put forward by the Greeley administration, to give $50,000 to BAWA. The BAC objected both to returning to GA annually for a reaffirmation of the commitment made in Cleveland and to the funding of BAWA.

At the 1969 GA in Boston, the Black Unitarian Universalist Caucus (BUUC), the membership organization that controlled the BAC, commandeered the microphones and demanded that the planned agenda be rescinded by vote of the delegates and replaced by a new one that put the BAC funding first. After an unusually bitter debate, delegates refused to accept this change. In response, many BUUC members left. Subsequently, those who supported them also left and regrouped at the nearby Arlington Street Church. A denominational schism seemed possible, but mediation was successful and the delegates came together again. Then, in a vote of 798 to 737, the delegates voted to support the BAC but not BAWA. . . .

Six months later, under a new president, Rev. Robert N. West, the UUA Board had to face the magnitude of the deficit and, understandably, reconsidered the association's budget, priorities, and commitments. A million dollars—40 percent of the budget—was cut, eliminating all twenty-one district executives and their offices, while the Office of Social Responsibility was combined with Religious Education to become the Department of Education and Social Concern. The Board focused more on survival than justice. Hard choices had to be made. Bearing responsibility for the institution's viability, the Board decided to spread the $1 million commitment to the BAC over five years instead of four. The BAC responded by disaffiliating from the UUA, and the 1970 General Assembly voted to stop funding the BAC, having distributed only $450,000 of the $1 million promised in 1968.[13]

More than four decades later, the anger and resentment that stemmed from the UUA's inability to take appropriate steps into the next phase of racial justice still permeate Unitarian Universalism. For many, the events and the broken relationships from that time remain unresolved, and their meaning remains uncertain. Even our name for this period in our history is a matter of ongoing debate. What is clear is that these events caused deep pain. The Unitarian Universalist community divided and lost important leaders and leaders-to-be when so many left. In the aftermath of this period, the UUA backed away from meaningful engagement in anti-racism work for several decades.

The 1980s and 1990s brought further changes related to issues of authority and the ministry of Unitarian Universalists of color. In 1982, the Commission on Appraisal published the report *Empowerment: One De-*

The UUA has continued to struggle with providing sufficient institutional support for ministers and seminarians of color. However, in recent years, the Association has begun another attempt at fostering healthy ministries for those who identify as people of color, Latino/a, Hispanic, and/ or multiracial/multiethnic.

nomination's *Quest for Racial Justice 1967–1982*, which suggested the Board appoint a Task Force on Racism. In 1988, the UUA's Department of Ministry Task Force on African-American Ministers developed the Beyond Categorical Thinking (BCT) program that has helped congregations envision hiring ministers from historically marginalized groups and is still in use today. In a 1989 study by the Commission on Appraisal on the "Quality of Religious Life in Unitarian Universalist Congregations," when asked if being African American would help, make no difference to, or hinder a minister's effectiveness, 3 percent of respondents considered it would enhance effectiveness, while 71 percent thought it would make no difference and 13 percent thought it would hinder effectiveness. However, the BCT program documented improvements in congregational responses to calling ministers of color after congregations participated in the trainings.

The late twentieth century also saw the beginning of new congregations, intentionally led by people of color and organized to serve those not served by existing UU congregations.[14] These were met with challenges of inadequate resources and tools from the UUA, as well as unrealistic expectations about how fast such congregations would grow. Rev. Rob Eller-Isaacs said that such congregational start-ups reflected the general challenges of institutional racism within the Association.[15] Likewise, issues of authority and ministry were cited in evaluations of attempts to establish congregational models that encouraged racial and ethnic diversity: Rev. Marjorie Bowens-Wheatley wrote that "it should be recognized that the lack of acknowledgment of a collective decision-making process within congregations is disruptive and unhealthy."[16]

The 1992 General Assembly in Calgary adopted the Racial and Cultural Diversity resolution, which brought about a series of gatherings related to anti-racism and transformed the lives of many UUA leaders. Unfortunately, these gatherings disconnected work on race and racism in the UUA from congregations.[17] Since then, identity-based organizations (such as the UU Network on Indigenous Affairs, UUNIA; Diverse Revolutionary UU Multicultural Ministries, DRUUMM; and Latino/a UU Networking Association, LUUNA) have been formed to serve members of various racial and ethnic groups in UU congregations, many of whom may have half a dozen or fewer people who look like them.[18] The Commission on Appraisal's report *Belonging: The Meaning of Membership* notes that "the tensions felt in congregational life for members of these [racial and ethnic] groups are similar to tensions arising from differing theological orientations, primarily the questions of who gets to define the culture of the congregation and the amount of diversity in style of worship and other programmatic areas of congregational life."[19]

The UUA has continued to struggle with providing sufficient institutional support for ministers and seminarians of color. However, in recent years, the Association has begun another attempt at fostering healthy ministries for those who identify as people of color, Latino/a, Hispanic, and/or multiracial/multiethnic. The Diversity of Ministry Initiative (DOMI) began operating out of the office of the UUA president in 2005. In 2008, DOMI hired a program coordinator as its first staff member. As of this writing, many of the initiatives of the Diversity of Ministry team are still in development. Its most successful endeavor to date is the establishment of a support network for seminarians of color and those who identify as Latino/a, Hispanic, Pacific Islander, Native American, Middle Eastern/Arab, and multiracial/multiethnic. This group meets monthly via teleconference, and in person when possible at General Assembly, the fall DRUUMM conference, and at specially organized retreats.

Another goal of DOMI was to assist congregations in an open and intentional dialogue about calling a minister of color. This was envisioned as a structured process backed by UUA funding and UUA staffing, designed to help qualified ministers from historically marginalized groups find settlements in larger "flagship" congregations. The DOMI tried to increase the likelihood of successful and lasting placements that would help transform participating congregations. Despite these efforts, there is currently some question about the future of the Diversity of Ministry Initiative.

Issues of ministry and authority in our congregations intertwine with the stories of anti-racism work within Unitarian Universalism. While many of these stories have not been documented, there are many resources available to deepen our understanding of these issues, such as the previous Commission on Appraisal reports mentioned in this chapter, the work of Mark Morrison-Reed, and *The Arc of the Universe Is Long: Unitarian Universalists, Anti-Racism, and the Journey from Calgary* by Leslie Takahashi Morris, Chip Roush, and Leon Spencer.

Women in UU Ministry

Following custom, the roles defined in the Cambridge Platform applied only to men within the congregation. Yet Universalist and Unitarian women have never been content to be silenced. Judith Sargent Murray helped organize Universalist conventions soon after the Revolutionary War. Gordon Gibson, who discovered her extensive papers, says, "She was a quiet leader in the establishment of organized Universalism and in the development of Universalist theology."[20]

Unitarian Maria Weston Chapman is best known as an abolitionist organizer. When the Congregationalist ministers of Massachusetts, reflecting the culture, issued a pastoral letter warning of the dangers of women speaking in public, she responded with a mocking poem that received wide distribution and comment.

Women began to assert themselves in the years following the Age of Reason. In England in 1792, Mary Wollstonecraft wrote *A Vindication of the Rights of Woman*. Judith Sargent Murray contributed to the discussion about education for women with an essay published in "The Massachusetts Repository" in 1797.[21] A Unitarian Transcendentalist and friend to Emerson, Margaret Fuller published her comments on women's rights in 1845 in her book *Woman in the Nineteenth Century*. During this period seeds were sown for new assertions on the part of women for rights they had long been denied. In 1839 in Mississippi, the Married Women's Property Act gave married women the right to own property. It was the first act of its kind. A more expansive law was passed in 1848 in New York State, aided greatly by the work of Elizabeth Cady Stanton, Paulina Wright Davis, and Ernestine Rose. Together with Unitarian Susan B. Anthony and others, these women struggled to change the course of women's lives. They were joined at various times by such progressive thinkers as Frederick Douglass and Universalist newspaper man Horace Greeley.

It's important to understand the intersection of progressive causes that many of these women worked on. Most were also involved in the abolitionist and temperance movements and struggled to bring them to fruition, together with progressive men of the day such as noted abolitionist and Unitarian minister Theodore Parker and Unitarian minister and promoter of women and Native Americans Samuel J. May.

In the second half of the nineteenth century, a small but determined group of women began to demand not just to be heard in congregations but to be allowed to lead them as ordained ministers. While doctrinal objections were rare within Unitarianism and Universalism, barriers of custom remained. In 1863, Olympia Brown was ordained by the Northern Universalist Association in New York. She went on to serve congregations in Massachusetts, Connecticut, and Wisconsin. Mary Augusta Safford and Eleanor Gordon, mentored by Rev. Oscar Clute, founded a Unitarian church in Hamilton, Illinois. They later moved to Iowa and trained young women to minister. Called The Iowa Sisterhood, these women founded and led congregations in several Midwest states. They were, however, exceptions to the mostly male ministry centered in the Eastern United States.[22]

In 1870, there were only five women who had attempted to serve among six hundred male liberal clergy; before the turn of the twentieth century, there were still only about twenty Unitarian or Universalist women clergy.[23]

Even when women began serving in ordained parish ministry, they were often only able to serve in congregations that were precarious in some way. Carolyn Owen-Towle, among the first Unitarian Universalist women to be ordained in the modern era, spoke about the challenges of leadership for women. In 1998, she called it "a tricky thing" and wrote that women have had to evolve into their natural leadership roles "as painstakingly as we used to work just to get what we minimally needed." She continued, "The fixation on female uppityness may be gradually fading, but it is still common enough to be ranked as a cultural disease. . . . Women who struggle long hours at low wages may be praised as virtuous or self-sacrificing. Somewhere on the way to the top, women are often mysteriously re-diagnosed as power-hungry and self-aggrandizing. The negative outcome is unwillingness on most women's parts to stick our necks out very far."

Further, Owen-Toole says, "Feminist thought has transformed our UU movement, revealing the systemic oppression of women by dominant male religious authority, through gender usage of God, the expression of worship, and church hierarchical structures. Gradually, these oppressions are being addressed, for feminist thought affirms the authority of women's experience and ultimate concerns."[24]

In a 1989 Commission on Appraisal study on the "Quality of Religious Life in Unitarian Universalist Congregations," when asked if being female would help, make no difference to, or hinder a minister's effectiveness, only 9 percent said that it would help, 78 percent said it would make no difference, and 13 percent said it would be a hindrance.

By the start of the twenty-first century, women were more numerous than men in Unitarian Universalist ministry. The culture had changed in several ways: Unitarian Universalists embraced diversity as a positive value and access to leadership via ministry as well as lay roles opened up to women and other minority groups. At the same time, responsibility for executive functions within congregations shifted from minister-led to lay-led in many churches, resulting in a reduction of the authority of ministers.

LGBTQ People in UU Ministry

The UUA's "Unitarian Universalist LGBTQ History and Facts" includes the following history of LGBTQ ministers in Unitarian Universalism:

> In 1969 the first UU minister came out as homosexual on the national scene: Rev. James L. Stoll. He never served a congregation again. Prior to that, ministers discovered to be gay were fired from their congregations (though once one was rehired as a custodian). In 1979 the first out gay men in the UU ministry were called to serve congregations: Rev. Douglas Morgan Strong, called to All Souls Church in Augusta, Maine, and Rev. Mark Belletini, called to First UU Society of San Francisco.
>
> In 1980, a General Assembly resolution urged the UUA to assist in the settlement of lesbian, gay, and bisexual religious leaders.

By the start of the twenty-first century, women were more numerous than men in Unitarian Universalist ministry. At the same time, responsibility for executive functions within congregations shifted from minister-led to lay-led in many churches, resulting in a reduction of the authority of ministers.

The UUA has been ordaining people regardless of sexual orientation since the 1970s, and the first openly transgender person was ordained in 1988.

In 2002, the first out transgender person in the UU ministry was called to serve a congregation: Rev. Sean Dennison, called to South Valley UU Society, Salt Lake City, Utah. Fewer than 5 openly transgender ministers have ever served UU congregations.

Today, about 5 percent of our ministers identify as lesbian, gay, bisexual, transgender, and/or queer. The UUA expects all ministers to show ministerial competency in the area of human sexuality before being approved for ordination. The UUA still has closeted lesbian, gay, bisexual, transgender, and queer ministers serving congregations and members in our congregations. People who are bisexual, queer, and/or transgender are more closeted in our congregations than those who are gay or lesbian. [25]

In a 1989 Commission on Appraisal study on the "Quality of Religious Life in Unitarian Universalist Congregations," when asked if being gay, lesbian, or bisexual would help, make no difference to, or hinder a minister's effectiveness, 2 percent thought it would help the minister, 33 percent thought it would make no difference, and 66 percent thought it would be a hindrance to their ministry. Around the same time as that study, congregations had begun to be encouraged to take the Beyond Categorical Thinking (BCT) trainings and pursue more inclusive thinking when it came to calling a new minister. More than fifteen years later, the UUA's Identity-Based Ministries Staff group determined that congregations that took the BCT training were nearly twice as likely to call a minister who identified with a historically marginalized identity (of race/ethnicity, sexual orientation/gender identity, or physical/mental disability) than those who did not take the training.

In writing this report, the Commission took care not to ignore the particular experiences of leaders claiming more than one marginalized identity, such as genderqueer people of color, who face extensive challenges to their authority within congregations. We will return to these experiences in later chapters.

Culture and Unitarian Universalist Aspirations

Given all of this history, we can see that Unitarian Universalist congregations in the United States are embedded in our national culture. We use Tema Okun's definition of culture from her book *The Emperor Has No Clothes*: "Culture is the set of values, beliefs, norms, and standards held by a group of people in order to insure the group's ability to operate." In other words, "culture is closely linked with power" and is often so embodied by those of us inside a culture that we do not see it.[31]

The national culture of the United States largely reflects the values, beliefs, norms, and standards of white dominant culture in a class-based society, and so our congregations have all been impacted by this cultural context.

Of course no culture can be completely summed up in words, and an exhaustive examination of white dominant culture is beyond the scope of this study. However, there are two features of white dominant culture which so impact our congregations' experiences of ministry and authority that we need to outline them here.

Hoarding authority: "Either/or" thinking is a feature of white dominant culture. This means that we often see authority as either in the hands of one person or group, or in the hands of another person or group. Therefore, we often feel that if one person or group has more authority or power, that necessarily means other people or groups have less. Further, we believe that resources are finite and therefore must be carefully apportioned. Many people in our congregations experience authority and power also as finite resources that must be carefully apportioned. This also inspires a wish that all decisions about authority should be made once and for all, and fixed for all time.

Individualism: In the pre-colonial and colonial periods, American culture was influenced by self-sufficiency and living in small, often isolated communities. The period of national expansion brought the ideal of the rugged individualist: the strong and healthy (normally white) male who was the captain of his life and the solo pilot in his social and economic affairs. These individualists believed in personal liberty, self-reliance, and limited interaction with institutions. In the late nineteenth and early twentieth centuries, an era of industrialization, United States culture was impacted by a free market economic system, strong profit goals, and maximization of individual wealth. Individuals rejected interference by government and support by institutions, including churches. An ethos of solidarity and collaboration was undermined by the belief that hard work alone determined a person's success and social worth, rather than inherited wealth and property as the markers of class privilege. Some of these rugged individualists were "free thinkers" who were associated with Unitarian or Universalist congregations. Their radical individualism often impeded the efforts of ministers and progress toward beloved community. We continue to experience the impact of rugged individualism in Unitarian Universalist congregations today.

Of course, our congregations are not only the products of national culture. They are also grounded in Unitarian Universalist aspirations, covenants,

The national culture of the United States largely reflects the values, beliefs, norms, and standards of white dominant culture in a class-based society, and so our congregations have all been impacted by this cultural context.

Our aspirations lead us in search of beloved community, covenantal relationships, and communities of wholeness and health.

and principles. Our aspirations lead us in search of beloved community, covenantal relationships, and communities of wholeness and health. In the ensuing pages we will dig deeper into these elements of congregational life. To begin, we must first address what we understand to be the primary concern of the congregation: its sense of purpose and the ways in which abstract faith transforms into concrete action. In other words, if we are to explore the complex relationship between ministry and authority, we must first ask: Just what is ministry?

Notes

1. Peter Hughes, ed., *The Cambridge Platform: Contemporary Reader's Edition* (Boston: Skinner House Books, 2008), 29.
2. Jack Mendelsohn, *Channing: The Reluctant Radical* (Boston: Skinner House Books, 1971).
3. David Bumbaugh, *Unitarian Universalism: A Narrative History* (Chicago: Meadville Lombard Press, 2000).
4. John A. Buehrens, *Universalists and Unitarians in America: A People's History* (Boston: Skinner House Books, 2011), 131.
5. Jean Ott, quoted in Mark D. Morrison-Reed, *Darkening the Doorways: Black Trailblazers and Missed Opportunities in Unitarian Universalism* (Boston: Skinner House Books, 2011), 229.
6. Peter Hughes, ed., *The Cambridge Platform: Contemporary Reader's Edition* (Boston: Skinner House Books, 2008), 25–26.
7. William R. Murry, *Reason and Reverence: Religious Humanism for the 21ˢᵗ Century* (Boston: Skinner House Books, 2007), 36–40.
8. Edith Fisher Hunter, "Sophia Lyon Fahs: Liberal Religious Educator, 1876–1978," accessed January 26, 2013, www.harvardsquarelibrary.org/unitarians/fahs.html.
9. Holley Ulbrich, *The Fellowship Movement* (Boston: Skinner House Books, 2008).
10. Pew Forum on Religion and Public Life, "Faith in Flux" (2009), accessed January 24, 2013, www.pewforum.org/newassets/images/reports/flux/fullreport.pdf.
11. Mark D. Morrison-Reed, *Black Pioneers in a White Denomination*, 3rd ed. (Boston: Skinner House Books, 1994), 214–215.
12. Paula Cole Jones and Mark D. Morrison-Reed, "David Hilliard Eaton," in *Darkening the Doorways: Black Trailblazers and Missed Opportunities in Unitarian Universalism*, Mark D. Morrison-Reed, ed. (Boston: Skinner House Books, 2011), 192.
13. Mark D. Morrison-Reed, "The Empowerment Tragedy," in *UU World* (Winter 2011), 29–35; adapted from Mark D. Morrison-Reed, "The Empower-

ment Paradox," in Mark D. Morrison-Reed, ed., *Darkening the Doorways: Black Trailblazers and Missed Opportunities in Unitarian Universalism*, Mark D. Morrison-Reed, ed. (Boston: Skinner House Books, 2011), 215–229.

14. Leslie Takahashi Morris, Chip Roush, and Leon Spencer, *The Arc of the Universe Is Long: Unitarian Universalists, Anti-Racism and the Journey from Calgary* (Boston: Skinner House Books, 2009), 38–44.

15. *The Arc of the Universe Is Long*, 39.

16. Marjorie Bowens-Wheatley, quoted in *The Arc of the Universe Is Long*, 40.

17. *The Arc of the Universe Is Long*, 103.

18. Commission on Appraisal, *Belonging: the Meaning of Membership* (Boston: Unitarian Universalist Association, 2001), 82–84.

19. *Belonging*, 84.

20. Sargent-Murray-Gilman-Hough House Association and the Massachusetts Foundation for the Humanities, contributors, *Judith Sargent Murray: Philosopher, Writer and Champion of Social Justice: Proceedings of a Conference* (Gloucester, Mass.: Sargent-Murray-Gilman-Hough House Museum, 1994), 20.

21. Judith Sargent Murray, *The Gleaner* (Schenectady, NY: Union College Press, 1992), 287.

22. *The Gleaner*, 501–502.

23. Cynthia Grant Tucker, *Prophetic Sisterhood: Liberal Women Ministers of the Frontier, 1880-1930* (Lincoln, Neb.: Authors Choice Press, 2000), 3.

24. Gretchen Woods, ed., "Leadership: Women's Impact on the UU Ministry," in *Leaping from our Spheres: The Impact of Women on Unitarian Universalist Ministry* (UUMA Center Committee, 1998), 91.

25. "Unitarian Universalist LGBTQ History and Facts," accessed February 5, 2013, www.uua.org/lgbtq/history/185789.shtml.

26. Tema Okun, *The Emperor Has No Clothes: Teaching About Race and Racism to People Who Don't Want to Know* (Charlotte, NC: Information Age Publishing, 2010), 4.

What Is Ministry?

Ministry within the context of the church has always been understood as actions performed as an outward sign of religious faith. In Christian scripture we find two key passages that answer the questions: What is ministry and who has the authority to perform it? The first comes at the end of the Gospel According to Matthew, in a passage known as the Great Commission:

> Now the eleven disciples went to Galilee, to the mountain to which Jesus had directed them. When they saw him, they worshipped him; but some doubted. And Jesus came and said to them, "All authority in heaven and on earth has been given to me. Go therefore and make disciples of all nations, baptizing them in the name of the Father and of the Son and of the Holy Spirit, and teaching them to obey everything that I have commanded you. And remember, I am with you always, to the end of the age."[1]

This passage is understood to establish apostolic succession within the Christian tradition, whereby the ministry of the Christian church is derived from Jesus' apostles and passed on to designated ministers chosen in succession (thereby establishing the ordained order of priests, bishops, etc.). This type of ministry is primarily a teaching one, concerned with transmitting the teachings of Jesus and the doctrines derived thereof by those deemed to be in apostolic succession. This has come to be known as a "ministry of the word."

Throughout the earliest days of church history, at least as transmitted in the Christian scriptures, this ministry of word and doctrine was of primary concern for the founding church leaders. However, as more and more people were baptized into this new community, further needs were brought to light as they tried to live within the bounds of doctrines. The earliest conflict in ministry is recorded in the Acts of the Apostles; it resulted from a doctrinal call to share and distribute goods, especially food, within the community. The distribution of food brought about a breakdown between the teaching and its practical application:

> Now during those days, when the disciples were increasing in number, the Hellenists complained against the Hebrews because their widows were being neglected in the daily distribution of food. And the twelve called together the whole community of the disciples and said, "It is not right that we should neglect the word of God in order to wait at tables. Therefore, friends, select from among yourselves seven men of good standing, full of the Spirit and of wisdom, whom we may appoint to this task, while we, for our part, will devote ourselves to prayer and to serving the word." What they said pleased the whole community, and they chose Stephen, a man full of faith and the Holy Spirit, together with Philip, Prochorus, Nicanor, Timon, Parmenas, and Nicolaus, a proselyte of Antioch. They had these men stand before the apostles, who prayed and laid their hands on them.[2]

In the Christian tradition, this establishes a ministry directed at personal care, a ministry of the body—what in certain religious orders is understood as the cura personalis, or "care for the person"—as opposed to the more spiritual ministry of the word. This ministry was to be performed by a new class of leader, the deacons, rather than the priestly class, leaving those serving within apostolic succession to tend to matters of the mind and spirit.

As the church progressed through history, this general understanding of categories of ministry, along with the division of labor, remained in one form or another. With the passage of time, however, have come some major shifts in understanding, both in what is entailed within the ministry of the body, and who holds the authority to perform this ministry.

A foundational precept of the Reformation movement, established within the writings of Martin Luther, is that of a "universal priesthood": a doctrine stating that every member of the church is responsible for teaching and expounding upon the Christian faith. Luther's justification came from his reading of the first epistle of Peter:

But you are a chosen race, a royal priesthood, a holy nation, God's own people, in order that you may proclaim the mighty acts of him who called you out of darkness into his marvelous light.[3]

For the first time, the tradition of apostolic succession was broken and the authority for the ministry of the word was spread wide. From this point stemmed the Protestant ideal of the "priesthood of all believers," though Luther himself never used that phrasing.

It was perhaps then a natural progression to move to having a priestly class ordained not from above, but called from within the body of the church by its members. In the Cambridge Platform of 1648, our Congregationalist ancestors distinguished between a preaching and teaching ministry, performed by a minister or ministers ordained by the congregation, as well as a more temporal ministry, which involved day-to-day governance and administration, performed by a select group of elders, who were also chosen by the congregation's members. Nearly a third of the Cambridge Platform addresses officers, officials, and just who, in fact, does what. The Platform establishes yet another category of ministry: what we'll call a ministry of governance.

Oddly enough, the Platform has little to say about the category of ministry of the body. While it explicitly states how the congregation is to care for and support its officers, there is little mention of how those charged with various ministries should in turn care for and support the congregation, outside of prayer and visitation of the sick.

More recently, we've experienced a further shift in what ministry means in church culture, at least in the United States. Over the last several decades, the rise of the so-called megachurch—churches with an average weekly attendance of over two thousand people—has expanded the definition of ministry. Within megachurches, ministry has come to mean any service offered by the church either to members or to the larger community. Scott Thumma of the Hartford Institute for Religious Research writes, "The image these congregations want to portray is 'This is your parents' religion, but bigger and better.'"[4] Thumma cites a church in Atlanta whose ministries include not only the traditional Bible studies and ties to missionary groups, but also "aerobics, karate, weight loss, and divorce recovery groups." Other churches even go so far as to provide ministries such as job training and automobile repair. Many of these congregations have a mall-like atmosphere, where a spiritual seeker goes for a one-stop shopping experience for all their needs, body and soul.

At the other end of the spectrum is the rise of the emerging church, a post-modern reform movement found especially among Protestant Evangelicals. While the common characteristics of emerging churches are hard to categorize, most are marked by a back-to-basics attitude toward Christian belief and practice, especially regarding their approach to worship and ministry. Emerging ministry is what some scholars call "praxis oriented"—concerned with how their faith is lived out (our basic definition of ministry, above). Members of emerging churches are concerned with following in the footsteps of Jesus, with right living (orthopraxy) more than right belief (orthodoxy), although belief still matters greatly. For many of the emerging churches, that right living is centered around the church's mission, defined by how humans may participate in God's redemptive work.

The other major development in recent history is the concept of shared ministry: the idea that the ministry of the church, whatever it may be, is taken up by both the professional clergy and the laity. While the concept may not be new, the nomenclature is indeed more recent. With the naming of the concept, congregations have begun a more explicit and concerted effort to put the idea into practice. Some churches have adopted a model of "gifts ministry," helping congregants identify ministerial gifts within themselves and opening channels to put those gifts into practice.

This is neither a comprehensive history of the practice of ministry in churches nor an exhaustive list of the ways in which ministry is practiced today. As this report looks into the state of ministry in our congregations, some, all, or in many cases none of these ideas of ministry come into play. However, hopefully this brief review of the concept of ministry in history provides helpful context to the larger atmosphere in which ministry develops and is put into practice in Unitarian Universalist congregations.

What Unitarian Universalists Are Saying About Ministry

We posed the following set of questions to many focus groups over the course of this study: We call some things, but not all things, that happen in our congregations ministry. What goes on in your congregation that you call ministry? Who does these things?

Interestingly, the answers to these questions did not vary significantly among the participants according to their roles within the congregation (minister, lay leader, religious educator, etc.), or their social locations (gender, race, sexual orientation, etc.). This was not the case with other sets of questions.

Almost universally, the initial response from focus group participants was that everything is ministry and we all do it. However, as the conversations progressed, the answers became more nuanced. For example, most respondents were reluctant to categorize things like the day-to-day maintenance of the building as ministry, at least not immediately.

Almost universally, the initial response from focus group participants was that everything is ministry and we all do it. However, as the conversations progressed, the answers became more nuanced.

I make a distinction between ministry and administration . . . tending the church building and functioning—that's not ministry.
　　—*"Katie," a lay member*

Another respondent put the source of this unease rather more bluntly:

What would trouble me is if everything is ministry, because then it is a completely useless word.
　　—*"Dick," a lay leader*

This was repeated in some form or another by several respondents. Unlike the megachurch notion of everything being ministry, upon further reflection some of our respondents were more than willing to draw a line.

We sometimes forget to make a distinction between ministry and marketing, and we have to be careful about that. When we are so focused on, for example, bringing people in or relating to some other group, we morph into something that is not us, so that we look like them, but we're not.
　　—*"Randy," a lay leader*

As respondents talked about what ministry is *not*, they seemed time and again to come back to a sense that the activities of the congregation, in and of themselves, are not necessarily ministry.

You can do committee work that feels like busywork and doesn't feel like ministry, and you can do the same work and it is ministry. It's about the approach to it; it's about the context of it, the way we think about the service that we're offering.
　　—*"Bob," a minister*

It occurs to me that what we define as ministry really, to a large degree, springs from personal commitment.
　　—*"Cathy," a director of religious education*

I would say that things in the congregation that are ministry are things that keep at the core, or center, heart, of the work of the greater good. So it's not actually about making sure the pancakes don't burn, but the whole reason why we're making the pancakes.
　　—*"Kristin," a committee chair*

Such responses suggest that ministry stems from the intentions and purpose behind the action. For some, this sense of purpose comes from the need for

"You can do committee work that feels like busywork and doesn't feel like ministry, and you can do the same work and it is ministry. It's about the approach to it; it's about the context of it, the way we think about the service that we're offering."
—*"Bob," a minister*

and ability to be spiritually fed by what one does.

> I think [ministry] is taking care of people's emotional, spiritual and psychological needs.
> —*"Sophie," a director of religious education*

> [Ministry is] serving others and ourselves in a spiritual way, or a practical way.
> —*"Jeff," a committee chair*

For others, the sense of purpose in ministry is rooted in the act of relationship building, specifically the building of relations within the community.

> I think ministry is the promotion of relationships and the depth of relationships and the welfare of the other person in the relationship.
> —*"Dick," a lay leader*

> Building relationships within the church and relationships outside the church with the community at large is ministry.
> —*"Drew," a parish minister*

Conversely, there was much discussion about activities that are specifically damaging to right relations in the congregation, and which are almost universally deemed not ministry.

> If you're a social club, you're doing just the opposite, you are excluding others. And I think that's the difference I see between ministry and things that go on that aren't ministry.
> —*"Derrick," a religious education committee member*

> I'm thinking there are processes that go on in congregations that are not [ministry], that undermine ministry. I'm thinking about gossip, the process of the way people communicate with each other . . . violent communication.
> —*"Saul," a parish minister*

Still others find their purpose in the call to serve one another. For them ministry has a vocational aspect.

> Everybody has different skills and everybody wants to feel needed and appreciated, and at the end of the day, everybody would like to feel that they had [ministered].
> —*"Nell," a director of religious education*

"Everybody has different skills and everybody wants to feel needed and appreciated, and at the end of the day, everybody would like to feel that they had [ministered]."
—*"Nell," a director of religious education*

For many of our respondents, the purpose of ministry is defined by the mission of the congregation. The intent of ministry is to serve not just the members or the community, but to advance the professed purpose of the church.

> [Ministry is] informed by our principles and mission statement. Ministry is anything you do with your church community that supports the mission of the work.
> —*"Claire," a congregation member*

> When we connect with each other intentionally to serve the mission and purpose of the church—what we have agreed to be our common mission and our common purpose—everything we do intentionally to promote that is ministry. . . . When individuals behave in a self-serving or ego-based action rather than for the purpose of the community or the congregation, that's not ministry.
> —*"Beth," a lay leader*

The idea of ministry as actions that serve a purpose was very common, but expressed in different ways. The most common of these was to say that ministry is comprised of actions which serve the congregation's mission. Other purposes that helped to make certain actions considered as ministry included service, vocation, and relationship building. Individual respondents often identified more than one of these as making a particular action a part of the ministry of the congregation.

The acceptance of the idea of ministry, however, was not universal. While some respondents—especially, but not exclusively, clergy—were reluctant to separate the term ministry from congregational activities, others were equally reluctant to use the word for anything the congregation did.

> I am a youth advisor, [but] I don't consider myself ministering to the youth. I'm just—I don't know—there for them. But I'm not a minister.
> —*"Christine," a lay leader*

> We are uncomfortable with ministry language. People object that they did not sign up for ministry.
> —*"Sophie," a director of religious education*

Some respondents noted intentional efforts within their congregations to lead the community into a broader understanding of ministry. A few of the congregations we encountered, working under the premise that everything is ministry, have taken to explicitly naming their working bodies as

"[Ministry is] informed by our principles and mission statement. Ministry is anything you do with your church community that supports the mission of the work."
—*"Claire," a congregation member*

ministries. For example, the *caring committee* has become the *caring ministry*. In some congregations that have tried this, the shift in nomenclature has resulted in a parallel shift in attitude and understanding among members.

> One kind of new thing that my church does is we don't have committees; they're all ministries: finance ministry and worship ministry. So in a sense all committee work is ministry because we're ministering to each other and the church as a whole. They make a real concerted effort to incorporate the new members into whatever fits their wants and needs. And it really helps to retain new members.
> —*"Laura," a director of religious education*

In other congregations, however, the experiment has been far less successful.

> At one point our congregation was trying to make everything ministry, and then that just confused everybody—the "parking lot ministry," and this, and this, and it just confused people. And so we backed off that.
> —*"Anne," a parish minister*

Although the terminology was not universal among our focus groups, the sense of ministry as something shared among clergy and laity was almost omnipresent.

> If we think of ministry as helping to take care of each other, that's how I define ministry.
> —*"Mary," a congregation member*

> What is ministry? I think it is caring; it is how we care for each other. That's ministry. Who does it? Everyone.
> —*"Renee," a committee chair*

We define ministry as service done as an outward expression of faith or values. This satisfies both tradition and the general commonalities expressed by the lay people and religious professionals we encountered in our study.

> An increasing amount of shared ministry is going on in [our] parish —lay and ordained both involved in teaching, adult education, social action, worship.
> —*"Joanne," a community minister*

It is impossible to deliver one all-encompassing definition of ministry in the congregational context, beyond something very general. For the time being, we will define ministry as service done as an outward expression of faith or values. This satisfies both tradition and the general commonalities expressed by the laypeople and religious professionals we encountered in our study.

However, that outward expression takes on many different forms and we are loathe to lift one above the other or rank them in any way. This would be a completely subjective exercise and would devalue the good work done by our congregations, whether it is understood by them as ministry or not.

Beyond our basic definition, we could also say that ministry is any act performed within the context of the congregation or any act that does one or more of the following:

- contributes to the spiritual wholeness of the person giving or receiving service
- advances the mission of the congregation
- taps into the deeper ministerial gifts of a person
- serves to deepen relationships between congregational members or between congregation and community
- deepens an individual or community in their faith or values
- keeps the physical entity of the congregation running in good repair
- keeps the health of the congregational system in good repair.

While the Commission is reluctant to name any sort of universal specifics regarding the meaning of ministry within the congregation, this by no means removes the burden of specificity from congregations themselves. This is perhaps the first and most vital step toward diminishing the probability and severity of conflict in our congregations due to the inevitable tension between ministry and authority.

In the pages to come, we will find that while conflict around ministry and authority manifests in different ways and to varying degrees, it frequently finds its source in a lack of explicit definitions and documentation of what needs to be done and who has the authority to do it. While we leave it to each congregation to determine what needs to be done, the question of who needs to do it is far more open and is the source of this relationship's complexity. As we shall see, there are various sources and forms of authority, and they fluctuate.

Notes

1. Matthew 28:16–20, New Revised Standard Version.
2. Acts 6:1–6, New Revised Standard Version.
3. 1 Peter 2:9, New Revised Standard Version.
4. Scott Thumma, "Exploring the Megachurch Phenomena: Their Characteristics and Cultural Context," accessed January 18, 2013, hirr.hartsem.edu.

What Is Authority?

It should come as no surprise that we Unitarian Universalists, who are the spiritual descendants of heretics, would have deep and abiding questions about authority. One of our earliest forbears, Michael Servetus, was burned at the stake by the Reformers of Geneva, Switzerland. His heresy was denying the Trinity and, by extension, the authority of the established church hierarchies. The quest to punish Servetus marked one of the rare instances of cooperation between Catholic and Protestant leaders during the period of the early Reformation.

Joseph Priestley, renowned as a citizen scientist, was a Unitarian minister who was accused of heresy for his views. He fled London for Pennsylvania, where he built a modest chapel and preached to a small congregation.

John Murray was fired from his English Methodist congregation after he began preaching the idea of universal salvation. He came to the United States to begin a new life away from the ministry, but was convinced to return to preaching and became "the father of American Universalism."

Just as we can find the basis of our questioning of authority in our history and theologies, so can we find the foundation for building the beloved community. Our Unitarian forebears embraced covenant as the basis for their faith; our Universalist forebears embraced a loving God as the basis for theirs. The two traditions are now united into a whole that is still evolving as a radically inclusive and loving faith.

What Unitarian Universalists Say About Authority

Out of the historical context of questioning authority among Unitarians, Universalists, and Unitarian Universalists comes the present understanding —or lack thereof—about authority within congregations. When we asked our focus groups to tell us where authority arises for ministers and laypeople in our congregations, we got a variety of answers. Here are examples of some common responses:

> There's this personal authority, by which we are called into professional ministry. There's this formal authority that we're granted in our letters of agreement or in our contracts. . . . There's sort of an informal authority in the church structure itself, [where] people grant us authority over aspects of their lives. [As in,] "Here, please, you are the authority—tell me what to do." Or, "Help guide me." Or, "Tell me, where do I go? Where's the light at the end of the tunnel?" But I'm also aware that there's another level . . . and that is, the authority by which we are named [or] titled; the authority by which we are credentialed. So, there's the ordination, there's the call, there's the settlement, but there's also the Fellowship Committee, which grants us, I think, a certain amount of some kind of authority that I can't quite stick my fingers into very well to get a hold of.
> —*"Diane," a minister*

> Obviously [ministerial authority] comes from the congregation. The congregation hires and fires the minister. There is that formal authority that may include or not include some formal requirements and contracts we sign with the ministers. Beyond that, a minister must bring to the congregation some professional training. That's why we have all of this complex process of vetting the ministers. Leadership also comes from character. The authority of the minister comes, in part, from their own background. To be a minister requires the ability to see outside of one's self, to see the needs of others, to see what's happening in the world. It requires compassion. It requires courage.
> —*"Randy," a lay leader*

> I was thinking in terms of those who have positions on boards that are actually voted on. The Board members are voted on by the congregation, so therefore, they have authority for decision making in Board meetings, for example. It actually comes through the congregation. I also think that it comes out of experience they have had. If

"The Board members are voted on by the congregation, so therefore, they have authority for decision making in Board meetings, for example. It actually comes through the congregation."

—*"Nell," a religious educator*

they've been on the Board, if they've been on a council, or chaired this committee, been there a long time, often that gives them the authority to have an opinion, and be heard and respected. And, hopefully, not money. [laughter] I think there are times when people who are worth a lot of money give the church some of it, and then think, with that, they have the authority to tell the minister which way to move, and say what decisions the congregation should make. That's sad.

—*"Nell," a religious educator*

Several of our interviewees also noted some difficulty even discussing authority within Unitarian Universalist congregations. Many congregations seem not to be having discussions about who has the authority to do what, at least not in sufficient detail.

Despite this confusion, our research has led us to a working definition of authority in Unitarian Universalist congregations: Authority is the ability to influence and bring about growth and change in an institution, or the ability to block and derail growth and change in an institution.

Authority and Power

While this working definition of authority is a sufficient starting point, it does not prepare us to discuss the delicate interplay between authority and power. For that, we turn to Dan Hotchkiss and his book *Governance and Ministry* to help us begin to understand the relationship between the two:

> The words *power* and *authority* overlap in meaning. *Power* as I use the word, means the ability to make things happen by legal right or other compulsion. The power of attorney, the powers of Congress, and the power that corrupts (or corrupts absolutely) are examples of the kind of power I mean. *Authority* is legitimate power. We appeal to authority to justify our power, and do things "by the authority" of others. When Jesus interpreted the Law, he spoke "as one with authority." . . . In English, the word *authority* comes from the same root as *author*, suggesting that authority might carry with it some creative license. When a board charges someone with fulfilling some aspect of the mission without specifying exactly how it should be done, it delegates authority.[1]

Power is used in many different ways in our congregations, sometimes with legitimate authority behind it and sometimes in opposition to legitimate

text continues on page 47

Our research has led us to a working definition of authority in Unitarian Universalist congregations: Authority is the ability to influence and bring about growth and change in an institution, or the ability to block and derail growth and change in an institution.

Composite Case Study 2

Profile

Congregation Name: Unitarian Universalist Congregation of Essex

Members: 340

City Population: 95,000

County Population: 300,000

Region: Central East

Professional Staff: Full-time Minister (Rev. Matthew Combs), full-time Director of Religious Education, quarter-time Music Director, part-time Office Administrator

The Situation

In 1997, the minister at the time felt strongly that the congregation should go through the process to become a Welcoming Congregation. He began to organize the effort, including calling together a committee to begin work. A slim majority of the Board supported the effort. Then several long-standing members of the congregation, including the couple who were the congregation's biggest donors, announced their objections to the program. This caused a huge controversy in the congregation and on the Board, and the work to become a Welcoming Congregation was abandoned. The minister ended up resigning, which was followed by roughly 20 percent of congregation members resigning their membership.

After several short ministries, a new minister, Rev. Matthew Combs, began to serve the congregation in 2003. By 2007, it was apparent that there was a growing desire among the members to restart the Welcoming Congregation process. Those who had the strongest objections in 1997 had passed away. This time, the process began by a vote of the congregation to start work. The vote was overwhelmingly in favor. Two years later, the congregation became a Welcoming Congregation. During this process, most of those who had left the congregation returned to membership.

The Board

A conversation about ministerial authority with the Board included the following exchange:

Mary: Well, that gets to, how much does a minister act on his or her own and how much is the minister engaged in shared ministry in the decision making? . . . That gets to one of my favorite quotes: "The people with a bad leader say we have a bad leader and the people with a good leader say we have a good leader and the people with a great leader say, 'Look what we have done.'" And that's what probably ministers learn—[that] it's not about them. It's about the health of their congregations.

John: In our congregation, every single time that we've ended up booting out the minister, it's been a battle of will or egos between the minister and the Board or the minister and the congregation. They butt heads at some point and the minister loses. And the ministers that really seem to be able to weather the rough spots and stick around when they want to stick around are very, very sensitive to the egos in the congregation, whether it's a body like the Board of Trustees or individuals, whatever it might be. And [they know] to not deliberately get in the path of those egos.

Mary: And have small egos themselves.

John: I have observed that you can have a very small ego with still a lot of self-confidence and that's a really, really good mix.

Eric: The true authority in my book would be to have no ego at all. To move beyond that to really convince people to look what you have done. Those are the great leaders. I think this other part of the question, "Where do you get your authority and how do they make their decisions about how they will do it?"— they have to decide that themselves. Humility is a real important thing for everybody.

John: There has to be some ego in there. If you have no ego, you have no opinion.

Later in the conversation:

John: [Here is] an example where I think our minister has been leading us, one of the things when he first came. It was a real eye-opener. Our minister, being new, would come to us and sometimes he'd get a thumbs-up and sometimes a thumbs-down. He didn't take offense. It's an ego issue. He'd come back the next month with a different idea. We've had ministers in the past who really would take offense if the Board didn't at least partially adopt any idea. That's a very, very different way of polity. [It's] the relationship between the minister and leaders that we've been really benefitting from the last nine years. It's also setting an example for those of us who are lay leaders. To see our minister and how he deals with these things really helps us, and ultimately serves us well.

When asked about stresses and strains and their relationship to differences of opinion about authority, the Board had the following exchange:

Mary: I would say our congregation does not like to be micromanaged by the minister. I think there's still a difference of opinion among congregants about the role of the minister. Should the minister be the CEO or not? The congregation does not like it when the minister makes a big decision and they are not part of it.

John: I agree. The answer is "some." I don't think it's a lot; it shouldn't be a lot. There's always going to be stresses and strains, because there's no way any minister could do a good job of all the things they're expected to do. There's things they're good at and things they're not good at, and hopefully they delegate to somebody else the things they're not good at. Because there's no way one person could do it all. [There are] bound to be stresses and strains in the sense that there will be differences of opinion [over] which ones the minister should concentrate on and which ones they should delegate of all the things a minister is supposed to do. And the same thing is true of authority. [Which] decisions do they consult us with and which decisions do they not consult us with?

I canvassed some long, long time members who were very unhappy with [the minister]. [They said]

"It's time for him to go!" Certainly that's not the general feeling in the congregation, so you know that's certainly an example of a stress and strain. Those people don't come to services. There's always going to be those kinds of stresses and strains, but ultimately people respect the wishes of the majority.

Eric: Democratic process.

John: It's not just one person, one vote; there's a tremendous amount of deference to how strongly a person or a small number of people feel . . . about a thing, but that five people will end up having a lot more influence . . . which I think is appropriate. So it's not just one person, one vote. That's how you get around trying to work with all the stresses and strains you're bound to have when you're trying to work with . . . the issues of authority and [the question] "What does ministry constitute?" Because it constitutes so many different things and you can have so many ways you can minister as a professional minister.

The conversation turns to the time of conflict in the past:

Eric: Well, all of that was before my time, so . . .

John: Fireworks! Fireworks!

Eric: When I came to the congregation it wasn't bad, it was good, . . . I think we do have stresses and strains, especially when you try to do new things. We're going to try to do more new things.

John: In terms of looking at the congregation, I know that because of our size we have been looking in some ways at how governance should be, which brings in the question of whether a minister should be a CEO or not. I wasn't aware that this was a business. The question—the conflict—is that there a lot of people in the congregation who are pretty competent and there are things we can do on a voluntary basis that we do not want the minister to have to do, because we want him to be doing ministerial things. There are certain kinds of decisions the congregation needs to make because they're the ones that have the authority to do that and the minister doesn't. That gets to the question of what are the opportunities that you miss if you're not well organized, if you don't have your governance structure in place to really take advantage of not only inviting more people in the door, but also going, "This is who we are, and this is the difference we intend to make in the world."

If you're not there you can't take advantage of that opportunity. You know, should we have some voice as a liberal religion? Those are questions that can create stress and strains. I like to call those growing pains.

Mary: We were like that too. Your identity gets wrapped up in what side you're on. We did a split and then we came back together. Most people came back.

John: It took ten years.

Mary: Some people came back right away. Some never came back, but most came back.

Eric: But ten years is a consequence of that kind of holding on to your opinion.

Interviewer: What other thoughts do you have about this?

John: I would just say that . . . we have increased our level of maturity as a congregation. We were at each other's throats so much because we really weren't dealing with these differences of opinion in an adult manner—more of a teenager or child manner—and hopefully most congregations realize eventually that there are different ways of handling difference of opinion.

Mary: We know what the brink looks like and we've been over the brink and now we look at the brink and we go, "No, no, no."

John: I'm not going there again.

Mary: It's not so important if it's going to drive us over the brink.

The Minister

A conversation with the minister about ministerial authority in the congregation included the following:

Rev. Combs: What I've learned is that the recognition by the congregation in the ministry, in the professional clergy, of an inner guidance of experience, of talents . . . that it's this recognizing process in congregations, that they affirm it's not just that they see it, [but] they have to find it; that it's something that they value, that's where we get our authority to go into making decisions about how to do it. And they still want to monitor [or] mess with [it], but it's the process of that recognition that is the power of authority that accumulates for us. It doesn't matter how much [a minister] comes in with or how great you think you are. [The congregation] recognizes what's happening.

I think maybe we forget what it's like to be a lay person. When I was a lay person in my Unitarian Universalist congregation, I would look at the minister, and he would wear a robe too, he would wear a robe in the pulpit and he had mystique, he had a mystique when he stood up there that was real. Even if he talked about stuff that I didn't agree with, when he stood up there and talked, that was a minister. So there is, we may not realize it, but there is authority for us too in our role. There really is. And you know, it comes up in an interesting way. One of the interesting things I have here is [the question of] what am I called. Am I called Matt, or am I Rev. Matt, and people are struggling with this.

Interviewer: Still?

Rev. Combs: Yeah, still. Still after nine years. Particularly the newer people in the congregation. They'll ask, "What should I call you?" and I struggle with it myself.

Interviewer: Now I ask you to turn your attention to the laypeople in congregations. What gives them the authority to make decisions that affect ministry in their congregations, especially the ministry carried out by professional clergy?

Rev. Combs: I think it's the same place we get our authority from. It's recognition by the congregation, so it emerges out of the congregation out of their experience. . . . They get that authority from somehow its being conferred in a recognition through the congregational process. I'm a mystical Unitarian in that

I see that there's an organic thing that happens in a congregation that has its own being and that being then confers the authority to serve, somehow. Which [happens] through the democratic process, but sometimes it's through inspired members of the congregation who are powerful leaders in the congregation who also facilitate that process.

I also think one of the sources of power in our movement is fear, that people who are afraid of change and particularly of upsetting the status quo sometimes are a strong power base in congregations. Often those people who are the matriarchs and patriarchs in the congregations—I can think of a number of congregations where those people constantly stand in the way of moving the congregation out of the social club mode and into a transformational community, because they're afraid that they'll lose their power and the minister will get too much power and then the identity of the congregation will no longer be under their control, so there are demonic dimensions to where power comes from in our congregations that we have to be extremely attentive to.

Money is another way that power accumulates for people. What they give. How involved they are. I can think of several members of our congregation who really are dedicated.

Interviewer: Where would you be without them?

Rev. Combs: Where would we be without them? But they accrue influence through how much they do.

The minister before me and the congregation had very different opinions about ministry and authority. And they had a horrible break up and negotiated resignation. My experience has been smooth sailing with no problems. So I don't understand how to parse that except that in my experience the congregation has very clear ideas about who does what and who doesn't do what . . . so the congregation is pretty unified in what they think about this. So the conflict was between the minister and the congregation. And maybe I'm compliant or something—I've accepted their definitions—but I find I can work effectively within their definitions so we haven't had a lot of stresses and strains around this, so I don't know. But I was thinking, but what about those others—and, in fact,

many of the ministries before us—maybe I'm devious, and I accumulated authority in secret when they didn't realize it.

Interviewer: What ideas do you have about how to overcome stresses and strains due to differences of opinion about ministry and authority?

Rev. Combs: Building trust. That that's the most valuable thing you can do to create some lubrication to allow the people to deal with their anxieties and fears and yet have a faith that the other person is not a horrible demon that I have to kill or drive out of the congregation to make the congregation safe for the rest of us. The more there's trust built between the minister and members of the congregation and between the members of the congregation and each other, that's really vitally important, and then also having it visible so that the trusting between the leadership of the congregation and the minister, they see the cooperation back and forth. The more trust people see happening, I think the more effectively you can deal with the stresses and strains—because you can't eliminate them. That's just who we are as human beings. At different levels.

Of course [systems theory expert] Edwin Friedman is who we go to about all this stuff. And I was looking at him, but he doesn't do it the way he—I think he's right because he's big on [the idea that] ministers must self-define and he always talks about that . . . in a disconnected way. When I think the key is, yes, you must self-define so people know where you are—what you stand for and what you think—[but] the other part that Friedman doesn't emphasize enough at all is that relationality where I want to hear where *you* [the congregation member] are, what you think, and even assist you in your own self-definition process so that you feel clear about where you are and you know that I honor that and that somehow both of us defining ourselves and hearing each other and honoring each other, that's where transformation can happen. That I can move and you can move when I honor where you are. But until I honor where you are, I'm not moving. Or until you honor where I am, then it's really tough to feel heard.

I think [the Center for] Nonviolent Communication gives a methodology that is so amazingly powerful. NVC is based on honoring the needs that people present and underneath a lot of our conflicts are a lack of recognition of the needs that are driving people, and when our needs are recognized and appreciated, again, that's the listening piece where I'm really in touch with—when you really know that somebody has heard what the need that's driving you is, it is transformational. The energy moves when you're heard, and so then you can move to a different place where when I understand you and honor you and you're honoring what's going on with me, then you can move to this different level of how do we move together in that mutual appreciation towards strategies. . . . Most congregations don't know how to do this work. They don't know how to organize themselves in a way to communicate with each other effectively. They know how to be in conflict with each other very well. They're very good at that.

Toward the end of the interview the minister adds:

Rev. Combs: You can have all the authority in the world but be powerless in the way that leads a congregation to act. . . . I grew up in a fellowship, and any time a minister started talking about power, little red flags go up; you know: "The minister needs to be tamed." So just to be able to have an open conversation about ministry and power is a wonderful thing.

authority. Beth Zemsky of One Ummah Consulting, using the work of social psychologists John French and Bertram Raven, posits five types of power: referent power, expert power, legitimate power, reward power, and coercive power.[2] This model is a helpful framework through which to discuss the ways power is used in Unitarian Universalist congregations. We also note two other types of power taken from other sources that pertain to the discussion of authority in the congregational context: religious vocation and power from the periphery.

Referent power: This refers to the power that comes from identification with, attraction to, or respect for a leader. If referent power comes from charisma without genuine integrity and strength from the leader, it is quite fleeting. But if it comes from high esteem for and identification with a leader who acts with integrity and genuine respect for others, it is a meaningful and lasting source of power.

Several focus group participants discussed personal characteristics that inspired congregations to grant authority to both ministers and lay leaders. These included personal presence, compassion, ethics, character, trust, and respect. Many respondents also noted that the relationship itself is an important source of ministerial authority.

> I think that ministerial authority comes from trust. I say that with the depth of wisdom of almost finishing seminary, so I'm fully open to being wrong once I get out there, but I really feel that is where it is from. If you trust someone, if someone trusts you, they are more likely to open to you and share with you and then when you ask the hard question, they are willing to sit with it more and not dismiss it.
> —"John," a minister

> I also think that laypeople get their sense of authority from their own personal code of ethics and from a sense of responsibility to be good neighbors within the congregation and within [something] larger.
> —"Joan," a lay leader

Expert power: This is power derived from specialized skills or knowledge which are either possessed by or perceived to be possessed by a leader. This includes not only technical knowledge but also the consistent ability to solve problems and give useful feedback, suggestions, or advice.

Expert power is granted to ministers on the basis of education and experience in ministry. Many focus group participants listed training and education as sources of ministerial authority. Others also saw the UUA's

"I think that ministerial authority comes from trust. If you trust someone, if someone trusts you, they are more likely to open to you and share with you and then when you ask the hard question, they are willing to sit with it more and not dismiss it."
—"John," a minister

credentialing process as a source of expert authority. Most lay respondents, however, did not demonstrate a clear understanding of what a minister's education entailed.

Despite this, several of our interviewees noted that Unitarian Universalist ministers may be granted less expert power than those ministers might expect, or that is granted to clergy of other denominations. One noted that people expect to be trusted in their area of expertise, but that trust doesn't always extend to ministers. One interviewee pointed out that laypeople are more willing to cede authority to a minister when they don't have the knowledge or experience themselves, such as when experiencing grief, the death of a loved one, a moment that calls for a rite of passage, etc. This suggests that when laypeople think they know more than the minister about something they don't cede authority, which may be the case in aspects of congregational life such as finance or staff supervision.

Ministers are not the only people in congregations given power and authority on the basis of knowledge and experience. This is true for lay leaders as well.

> Authority does not always attach to specific committees within the lay leadership . . . so what makes the difference then? I think [things] like how long they've been an ongoing, faithful presence in the community, how reliable they are, [and] the quality of what they contribute.
> —*"Sally," a lay leader*

Legitimate power: This is the power that derives from holding a leadership position in a group or organization. It includes all of the formal structures and documents which grant authority both to ministers and laypeople.

> It is my role as the person who has been called to ministry by something larger, and as the trustee of the sacred office of minister that has been handed down for millennia . . . to maintain certain standards and to be involved, and to evoke the greater, the holy, the larger, the Spirit of Truth, in everything that happens in the life of the church. That is my job as the spiritual leader of the church.
> —*"Chuck," a minister*

Some of the power that comes with a particular role or position within a congregation has been agreed upon by the congregation itself and is embedded within its systems. However, this category also includes the ways people are granted differing degrees of authority within certain systems of power, privilege, and oppression. These systems give power to some groups over others, and provide easy access to power for some people, while leaving

"Authority does not always attach to specific committees within the lay leadership . . . so what makes the difference then? I think [things] like how long they've been an ongoing, faithful presence in the community, how reliable they are, [and] the quality of what they contribute."
—*"Sally," a lay leader*

others without this access. Those who find they have less access to power include young ministers, women in ministry, LGBTQ ministers, and ministers of color in our institutions.

> So often at the UU table, it's fake authority [which] is given. And if we start thinking that we are all that because we've been chosen, without understanding the wider context of the racism that continues to exist . . . [it suggests that] the old boy's network, the old girl's network, the old cousin's network—whatever you may want to call it— . . . is alive and well . . . and . . . thriving.
> —*"Helen," a minister*

> I believe that the minister or clergy, or that person who talks a lot . . . gets their power from anyone over thirty.
> —*"Dina," a youth member*

Dina and Helen reference the ways in which adult privilege, as well as white or class privilege, determine the ways power is structured. We will have much more to say about this in the next chapter when we address who has authority and who does not.

Reward power: This is the power that comes from the ability to give people something they want, such as access to the minister. However, we did not find that this was a major source of power and authority among ministers and laypeople within Unitarian Universalist congregations.

Coercive power: This is the power to coerce or punish if one's expectations are not met, including by withholding emotional support or tangible resources. Many people in our focus groups and interviews noticed the distinct lack of coercive power among Unitarian Universalist clergy. Our studies revealed that this is a type of power that, when brought into play, is usually wielded by laypeople.

Some ministers within our focus groups felt that there are particular contexts in which their ministries can be destroyed by one person or a small group of people—for example, when people have the power to fire a minister in reality even if they don't have that power in theory.

> Before I was called to [my congregation], both the interims shared that one woman in particular had been identified [as] the person who held the most power in the church—a layperson. So, I've made sure that she and I have a fabulous relationship, because she does— she has the power to make or break my ministry.
> —*"Diane," a minister*

"The old boy's network, the old girl's network, the old cousin's network—whatever you may want to call it—is alive and well and thriving."
—*"Helen," a minister*

One of the principal ways coercive power can operate in Unitarian Universalist congregations is in the threat of withholding pledge income.

> [Our congregation] tried to become a Welcoming Congregation a number of years ago and for whatever factors, it didn't happen. . . . Large contributors back then didn't support it. That's a big reason why it didn't happen.
> —*"Ted," a Board member*

Religious vocation: Some of our focus group participants identified power that comes from a religious vocation or call, which some experience as coming from God or from a divine source, while others experience it as a personal inclination or impulse toward ministry. This is most often applied to ministers, though some participants mentioned call or vocation as a source of lay authority as well. Uniquely in this arena, we found some participants explicitly asserting authority from a religious vocation, while other participants explicitly denied that this sort of authority operates in our congregations.

> I draw my authority from several sources . . . one [is] my colleagues, . . . the second is the congregation itself, . . . and the third, however anyone wants to describe it, is a higher power, god, goddess. I do think I am accountable to a higher sense of myself, something beyond me, and I think that there is wisdom from a transcending mysterious force, and that we can't just rely on what is immediately in front of us.
> —*"Jude," a minister*

In a hearing during General Assembly in 2011, a participant said, "I have, through the mentoring of my elder colleagues, come to conclude that the first source of authority is a call from God." This comment elicited hisses from another participant.

In a hearing during General Assembly in 2011, a participant said, "I have, through the mentoring of my elder colleagues, come to conclude that the first source of authority is a call from God." This comment elicited hisses from another participant.

Power from the periphery: Coined by womanist theologian Rosita deAnn Mathews, this is a form of personal power that challenges the established or dominant standards of power embedded in systems of oppression and abusive institutions.[3] This type of power gives people at the margins, such as people of color, women, youth, and LGBTQ people, the ability to resist discrimination, exclusion, or injustice. Peripheral power interrupts the assumptions operating as legitimate power in an organization, offering an alternative paradigm for historically marginalized individuals and groups to act authentically and ethically.

In our focus groups, ministers who are marginalized in various ways described an impulse to claim a certain power from the periphery, whether that power is recognized in the system or not, and operate from that place.

> I was doing ministry, whether the fellowship I was working with would grant me that or not. So, there's something beyond.
> —*"Diane," a white minister*

> I'm so adamant and feel so strongly about claiming our ministerial identity. If we wait for them to give us authority and identity, a lot of us will be dead and gone. If we claim it, we're still going to have the problems of being the person of color in the white congregation. But, if I claim it, you can't take it away from me.
> —*"Donna," a minister of color*

All these types of power and authority exist in Unitarian Universalist congregations, and this discussion points to their many sources.

Authority from Congregational Covenants

Ultimately, the foundational sources of authority in Unitarian Universalism and in Unitarian Universalist congregations are our covenants. Alice Blair Wesley, in her Minns Lectures on covenant within Unitarian Universalism, tells us that authority in Unitarian Universalist congregations comes from mutual promises among individual congregation members. Authentic authority comes only from the members, not from a hierarchy or central office. Authentic authority among congregations springs from the relationships among individuals in the various congregations.[4]

This idea is borne out by our focus group participants. They disagreed about many things, but the one idea we heard more than any other was that the source of authority for ministry in Unitarian Universalist congregations comes from the congregation itself. This was not only asserted by the vast majority of our focus group participants, both lay and ordained, it is also something that matters deeply to many of the participants.

> Members could vote on whether or not we were going to accept this minister and offer her the position. . . . I felt it was as democratic as possible with such a big group . . . so it was really powerful. . . . The clergy, I feel, gets the power from the congregation that really chooses to give them that power and gives them that role, as a facilitator really, for the congregation or church.
> —*"Melissa," a youth member*

"I'm so adamant and feel so strongly about claiming our ministerial identity. If we wait for them to give us authority and identity, a lot of us will be dead and gone. If we claim it, we're still going to have the problems of being the person of color in the white congregation. But, if I claim it, you can't take it away from me."
—*"Donna," a minister*

This sense that the congregation is the ultimate source of ministerial and lay authority—when it is grounded in the power of covenantal living—can empower congregations and their leaders to do ministry in healing and transformative ways.

This sense that the congregation is the ultimate source of ministerial and lay authority—when it is grounded in the power of covenantal living—can empower congregations and their leaders to do ministry in healing and transformative ways. However, the notion that all authority derives from the congregation can also lead to conflict and crisis if a congregation lacks an understanding of covenantal relationship and sees authority as something that can be snatched away at any time. An overemphasis on the importance of individualism can lead to authority being both granted and withheld in harmful ways, which can especially affect those who are most vulnerable due to their location in the congregation or in society. Knowing the source of authority, then, is not enough to allow us to address its complexities. To gain a fuller picture of congregational authority, we must understand the ways in which it is channeled and the hands that wield it.

Notes

1. Dan Hotchkiss, *Governance and Ministry: Rethinking Board Leadership* (Herndon, VA: The Alban Institute, 2009), 200.
2. Beth Zemsky, "Types of Power," adapted from John French and Bertram Raven, "The Bases of Social Power," in D. Cartwright (ed.) *Studies in Social Power* (Ann Arbor: University of Michigan, 1966), 150–167.
3. Rosita deAnn Mathews, "Using Power from the Periphery," in *A Troubling in My Soul: Womanist Perspectives on Evil and Suffering*, ed. Emilie Townes (Maryknoll, NY: Orbis Books, 1993).
4. Alice Blair Wesley, *Our Covenant, The 2000–2001 Minns Lectures* (Chicago: Meadville Lombard Theological School Press, 2002).

Who Has Authority and Who Does Not?

Unitarian Universalism is a faith thoroughly grounded in the history and culture of the United States. Our roots are Abrahamic, transferred through Reformation Europe, especially England. However, Unitarianism and Universalism were nourished in the revolutionary atmosphere of the colonies and formed alongside our nation itself. As such, Unitarian Universalism reflects our nation's cultural characteristics, both positively and negatively. Thus, our congregations reflect the continuing tension between two basic values: rugged individualism and community. The idealized conquerors of the frontier were individualists, while the developers of our democracy valued community and worked together to build our nation state and its institutions. Both characteristics were and are necessary.

The tension between individualism and community is often exhibited within our congregations, especially when they struggle over questions of authority. For example, lay members who value rugged individualism might join with others of the same mind in factions, who are very sure that their understanding of what needs to be done is the one and only way forward. Others who are community centered might join together as well, leaving the congregation with competing power sections. Disagreements escalate into conflicts. The factions adopt a "my way or the highway" approach. The resident patriarch(s) and/or matriarch(s) may be recruited to—or may lead—one side of the conflict. As the informal leaders or "parents" of the congregation, they may be sure they know best what should be done. The two sides fail to cooperate while performing the ministries of the congregation. The sides may stake out turf, such as religious education for children, social action programs, or control of the worship service. Areas of programming or maintenance may get neglected.

In such power struggles, it is very difficult and probably impossible for ministers to remain uninvolved. Regardless of identity and experience, ministers spend a majority of their time and energy struggling with the questions of authority that rise from the tension between individualism and beloved community.

This is not the only example of a power struggle over a congregation's operations and ministries. There are many ways in which the cultural expectation of limited power and authority come into play.

When tensions arise in the congregation, who are the common parties? Who has authority in these situations? Of course, there are people in every congregation who have formal authority over various aspects of congregational life—the Board, committees, staff, and professional ministers. However, as we heard from our focus group participants resounding in near consensus, formal authority is never the only kind of authority in congregations, and often it is not the most powerful kind.

As we heard from our focus group participants resounding in near consensus, formal authority is never the only kind of authority in congregations, and often it is not the most powerful kind.

Most churches have longtime members, maybe even church founders, who could be described as patriarchs and matriarchs. These roles are not inherently bad. They are necessary and worthy of honor and recognition. However, the power these individuals hold is out of balance with that of other members of the congregation or the minister. Further, the roles they hold are not available to everyone. In Unitarian Universalist congregations these roles are almost always held by white heterosexual couples and are almost never available to younger people, queer people, working class people, or people of color.

Even elected leaders in congregations lack authority in some situations. One of our interviewees told us a story he had heard from a female Chinese American Board president. She described how white ministers and congregational leaders have had a particularly strong impact on the roles available to people of color. When she spoke to other congregational leaders about growing in diversity as a congregation, she heard a typical response from her white fellow congregants: "You're a nice Chinese woman, but my school was all Chinese and I would like to get away from all the Chinese [while at church]. I like it here because there are more people like me." When the Board president brought her concerns to her white minister for counseling, she encountered pushback from the minister. He told her that she was "over-emotional and sensitive." Our interviewee reflected that there is a history of white male ministers accommodating the anxieties of congregations about engaging difference.

Many congregations break into factions during conflicts. These factions can become power bases that can challenge the authority of those who, in theory, are in charge of various aspects of congregational life. Sometimes these factions can become so strong that they are a sort of second board, the place where "real decisions" are made which can undermine official decisions of the official governing Board.

Ministers and formal lay leaders would be wise to call upon available resources to assist them as they lead their congregations back toward the center: the balance point between individualism and community; the place where individuality is not lost, but members unite into a whole that values each person.

Theological Differences

In addition to the tension between competing values, Unitarian Universalist congregations also contain theological differences. We claim to be theologically inclusive, but living out our aspirations is more difficult than stating them. In a cultural context that sees authority as a finite resource, we struggle to define what will be the dominant theological and worship experience in our congregations. The classic tension between humanists and theists is enlivened by the addition of pagans and Buddhists as well as the occasional Muslim or Hindu.

A participant in the Commission's hearing at the 2011 General Assembly shared this story:

> While I was on the Board [of my congregation] I was a member of CUUPS [the Covenant of Unitarian Universalist Pagans], and I was very careful to not let my spiritual philosophy interfere with my Board duties. However, our minister at the time was very clear that pagans had no spiritual authority in the Unitarian Universalist Association.
> —*"Wanda," a former Board member*

Theological differences within our congregations often manifest in struggles to control the worship service. For example, humanists who join our faith after leaving a more traditional Judeo-Christian congregation sometimes want to reject any reminder of that tradition. They tell ministers that "God language" is unacceptable, or that they may not "pray" or deliver a "sermon," and instead may give a "talk" or "speech." "Meditations" are acceptable, though the term may confuse the Buddhists who understand it to mean something different.

When paganism first emerged, humanists and theists united in regarding it as a threat to Unitarian Universalist congregations. However, pagans prefer to worship in nature, and in most congregations they moved their

We claim to be theologically inclusive, but living out our aspirations is more difficult than stating them. In a cultural context that sees authority as a finite resource, we struggle to define what will be the dominant theological and worship experience in our congregations.

seasonal celebrations to non-Sunday morning times and often non-church venues. They do not often control the regular Sunday morning worship service and are therefore actually less of a threat.

Having learned from current research that the "nones" (current language for those who are unchurched) are looking for a spiritual experience in our congregations, Unitarian Universalist ministers find themselves in the midst of another major challenge to their authority. This challenge is leveled at the core task of ministry. If ministers, the trained professionals, do not have the authority to craft the worship experience to the best of their ability, they cannot perform their task.

Unitarian Universalist Values

Because United States culture influences our congregations and undermines our search for beloved community, it also undermines our Unitarian Universalist values. The 2005 Commission on Appraisal report, *Engaging Our Theological Diversity*, revealed that most of our congregations used the UU Purposes and Principles as a theological document. It also showed that promises and covenant were critical to our contemporary theological understanding of the faith. From the seven Principles and the six Sources, the Commission in 2005 identified the following five promises as "our foremost covenantal commitment to living the interdependent web":[1]

- We promise to live relationally.
- We promise to live ethically.
- We promise to live pluralistically.
- We promise to live evangelistically
- We promise to live globally.[2]

The report also noted:

> Each church member brings a different understanding of the UU faith into his or her religious community; each brings a different hope for how to experience religious and spiritual life. One theology cannot fit every kind of Unitarian Universalism today. Within the UU religious movement, which embraces a spirit of questioning and daring, permeates a strong and steady fear of "the other." It is not easy to have that which we call dear threatened by "the other" either.[3]

We find hope by encouraging our members to embrace completely the value of hospitality, working to engage our young people, and lifting up the

Purposes and Principles that we profess to promote. Our Unitarian Universalist Principles and aspirations can provide the counterbalance to the cultural assumption of finite theological authority. We can return to an understanding that our congregations can be places that nurture theological diversity.

When we promise to live in this way, inspired by frequent reading and repeating of our Purposes and Principles, we tend to believe that we are already doing so. It is difficult to see when we are falling short of these aspirations. We think we are cooperating, when in fact we are hoarding power. We think we are accepting when we are not. So we fall back into the trap of guarding our power which we perceive as a finite and precious resource and forget our Principles. We hold only one cultural model of leadership, and forget that there are other, more cooperative models.

Cultural Standards for the Minister

Into this complex mix of high ideals and cultural shortcomings comes the modern day Unitarian Universalist minister. How can today's minister establish credibility? How can the congregation draw upon the minister's strengths without losing its identity? What does the congregation expect? The following story by Clinton Lee Scott was told by Rev. Michael Schuler at the Service of the Living Tradition in 2011.

> Now it came to pass that while the elder in Israel tarried in Babylon, a message came to him from a distant city, saying, come thou and counsel with us. Help us to search out a priest, for the one that has served us has gone mad. And the elder in Israel arose and journeyed to that distant city. And when the men of affairs were assembled, the elder spake to them saying, What manner of man seeketh thee to be your new priest? And they answered and said unto him, We seek a young man yet with the wisdom of gray hairs. One that speaketh his mind freely, yet giveth offense to no one. That draweth the multitude to the temple on the Sabbath but will not be displeased when we ourselves are absent. We desire one who has a gay mood yet is of sober mind. That seeketh out dark sayings and prophecies yet speaketh not over our heads. That filleth the temple, buildeth it up yet defileth not the sanctuary with a motley assortment of strangers. We seeketh one that puts the instruction of the young first but requireth not that we become teachers. That causeth the treasury to prosper yet asketh not that we give more of our substance. Verily we seek a prophet that will be unto us a leader but will not seek to change us, for we like not to be disturbed. And the elder in Israel answered

We think we are cooperating, when in fact we are hoarding power. So we fall back into the trap of guarding our power which we perceive as a finite and precious resource and forget our Principles. We hold only one cultural model of leadership, and forget that there are other, more cooperative models.

and said unto them: When I have found such a priest I will indeed send him unto you, but you may have to wait long, for the mother of such a one has not yet been born.[4]

This story has been changed, modified, and modernized. It is frequently used by ministerial settlement representatives when they train search committees. We laugh at it ruefully, for we recognize the element of truth that makes it so effective. We all want a minister who will preach with power, guide us with grace, share deep wisdom with humility, and love us unconditionally. As the elder said, the mother of such a one has yet to be born. Ministers are also human and therefore imperfect.

In a culture that contains the tensions described above, it can be difficult for congregants to grant power to ministers. We have heard from focus group participants, interviewees, and ministerial settlement representatives that congregations not only have impossible expectations of the practice of ministry, but also hold a certain cultural standard of who a minister is. We heard over and over that those who are closest to this cultural standard are more likely to be granted power and authority. If the minister's characteristics do not fit this standard, their authority may be compromised. One focus group participant put it this way:

> My notion is that people of color in this denomination, professional clergy, cannot get authority unless they demonstrate sufficient closeness to middle class, Harvard-graduated, white men, who are sixty years old. And that's the model. And you cannot get authority unless you approximate that model.
> —"William," a minister

Transgender/genderqueer people are also vulnerable to having their authority compromised because they do not fit this cultural standard. One minister who identified as transgender testified that while it seemed unimportant when settling into the congregation, when a problem later arose, there was great reluctance to trust or grant authority to the minister. We have also found that many search committees are reluctant to even talk about gender identification.

Ministers with disabilities also report experiencing a lack of authority, as do younger and older women. An older female minister told of her surprise at being perceived as available for "patting." Her formerly strong personal boundaries were erased by what were meant to be affectionate gestures: pats on the head or back, hand holding, etc. She understood that her authority had evaporated with her last birthday. Young women in ministry often report frequent comments on their appearance, including clothing and hairstyle.

"My notion is that people of color in this denomination, professional clergy, cannot get authority unless they demonstrate sufficient closeness to middle class, Harvard-graduated, white men, who are sixty years old. And that's the model. And you cannot get authority unless you approximate that model."
—*"William," a minister*

We heard clear examples of the differences in how congregations grant men and women ministerial authority from our focus group of co-ministers, most of whom were serving in a co-ministry situation with someone of a different gender. Most participants in this group agreed that the men in their co-ministries were given more authority than the women. The following is an instructive exchange.

"Beth": Being a part of a male-female co-ministry team . . . I know that [we] really do have to struggle around that because people give him more authority than they give me.

"Mike": That's absolutely right.

"Beth": You know, because the culture says that he looks more like a minister than I do and that's been an ongoing dynamic in co-ministry we have to just constantly address.

However, one participant also noted that she is seen as a less threatening source of authority than her male co-minister.

I think there are some situations where congregants have given him more authority than me. But I also have experienced people who have trouble with authority having more trouble with Jeff than with me, even though we're exerting very similar kind of authority. So, if he comes to a meeting with an idea, sometimes people will take it more heavily even though he is a very soft spoken guy, and then they'll sort of rebel against him in a way that they wouldn't necessarily do with me.
—*"Sarah," a minister*

A minister who closely approximates the cultural standard has only to prove they are ministerial enough, while those on the periphery have more to prove to be considered an effective minister. The process of proving oneself effective is harder for those working against assumptions based in racism, sexism, and/or ageism. One young minister reported often being told, "You are very wise for someone so young." A participant in a focus group of ministers of color talked about having to overcome racialized assumptions about their expression and abilities.

Once you demonstrate that you can write, and people can understand what you have to say, and it's coherent when you preach and you don't show too much emotion, and you don't make people uncomfortable, then you can gain some level of authority.
—*"William," a minister*

Ministers usually establish long-term credibility by developing deep pastoral relationships. When those are in place, the minister can weather the congregational storms. However, when ministers are unable to do so because congregants do not identify them as ideal for their role, they are not granted authority. Ministers who vary in some degree from the cultural standard also find that authority that is given is often quickly revoked.

> You can gain some level of authority, but that level of authority is veneer thin because you never know when it's going to be snatched back because you've made somebody more uncomfortable than they were prepared to feel.
> —"William," a minister

Participants also told us that they notice that congregations are particularly uncomfortable with individuals who don't exactly fit one of the marginalized categories, so there is additional pressure on marginalized people to fit into one easy-to-define category.

> In terms of communities of color, if you're going to be Hispanic, you need to be Hispanic; you can't be Cuban-American, or whatever. You need to fit one category, and we don't. And it's messy and it's beautiful and it's complicated, but that's reality. We're not one thing. And we should not be forced to live in the constraints of just one thing.
> —"David," a minister

The Power Network

In addition to congregations, colleagues also give ministers more or less authority based on their approximation to the cultural standard of the white, heterosexual, middle-aged male. Power is held by the "old guard" and tends to operate covertly. Ministers for whom the cultural standard is too narrowly configured are not supported by collegial leaders, and thus, more vulnerable in congregations.

In a focus group of ministers of color, participants noted that authority comes from the relationship of ministers to their colleagues and within the denominational infrastructure, or the web of leaders who bestow authority upon one another. One participant noted that the authority given to ministers of color in this collegial web is "fake" because their professional and ministerial identity is lost in the broad context of racism.

Participants noted that people of color can become "flavors of the year" and given false power if they demonstrate a willingness to support those in power and the status quo of class, gender, speech, and education that allows one to assume authority. They are often seen as representatives of a specific ethnicity and must always be "on," though this comes with some access to policy-making conversations. Yet authority or power is often snatched back if, as one participant put it, they "make people more uncomfortable than they were prepared to feel." So, people who have been called upon association-wide as the "flavor of the year" may find themselves without support and no longer included in conversations.

Potential allies may have little idea how to live out their desire to support their colleagues when authority is suddenly "snatched back." They often do not have a reference point for these experiences of "fake" power and its sudden withdrawal.

And so it is that the authority to perform ministry, to put the faith of our communities into action, is complicated by the very human hands that wield it. False expectations, prejudices, old wounds, and ancient grudges stand in the way of authority and stem the flow of power in service to our ideals. The relationship between authority and ministry is complex, quite simply, because we are.

Conflict over authority is inevitable. The question is not how to avoid it, but how to adjust the environment so that power can flow where it must. Our final two chapters examine what these conflicts look like and what our congregations can do to more easily navigate the complex ground over which authority flows.

The authority to perform ministry, to put the faith of our communities into action, is complicated by the very human hands that wield it. The relationship between authority and ministry is complex, quite simply, because we are.

Notes

1. Commission on Appraisal of the Unitarian Universalist Association, *Engaging Our Theological Diversity*, (Boston: Unitarian Universalist Association), 129.
2. *Engaging Our Theological Diversity*, 123–131.
3. *Engaging Our Theological Diversity*, 117.
4. Clinton Lee Scott, *Parish Parables* (Boston: Beacon Press, 1946).

Conflicts About Ministry and Authority

Patterns of conflict became apparent as we talked with people from congregations. We are not referring to disagreements that can be resolved relatively easily, but rather those that grow into ongoing conflicts that damage congregations' spirit and ministries, and split congregations. It is important to understand the ways in which authority is acquired or lost, as that process is often either at the heart of a conflict or is a causality of the conflict.

Here again, we on the Commission see a tension between our Unitarian Universalist aspirations and a cultural context that leads to conflicts over authority and power. Given our Unitarian Universalist covenant—our Principles—why do so many congregations have conflicts regarding authority and leadership? We Unitarian Universalists respect the worth and dignity of individuals, yet we behave disrespectfully toward ministers and lay leaders. We support justice and compassion in human relations, yet we often scapegoat our ministers. We accept each other and encourage each individual's spiritual growth until someone speaks out about their different spiritual path. We promote a free and responsible search for truth and meaning, yet we resist changes from the way things have always been. We follow a democratic process, yet small power groups often work behind the scenes in our congregations. We claim a goal of world community with peace, liberty, and justice for all, yet within our congregations we often find conflict and inequity. We respect the interdependent web, but the web of relationships in our congregations often resembles a tangled, thorny mess. How do we get into situations like this and how do we navigate away from them?

Many of the stories we heard through our focus groups and interviews, like our composite case study on page 42, lead us to ask what it is about our church culture and the culture around us that undermines our ideals, and more important, what we can do about it. It is equally important to ask why some ministers, lay leaders, and members are more affected than others by the systemic causes of our conflicts.

The problems with authority are both situational and systemic. They are both uniquely different and they follow patterns that appear again and again. Some relate to human behavior and others are a result of the structure of our congregations. Some have deep historical roots while others have newer origins.

When we asked our focus groups what ministry is and who does it, the discussion enlightened us about conflicts over authority issues. As we saw in the chapter "What Is Ministry?," there is a wide divergence in the understanding of ministry and ministers. The recent proliferation of the term "shared ministry," applied to many situations, has robbed the term of its meaning and led to confusion over governance and ministry, worship and ministry, and service and ministry. This confusion often contributes to conflicts over authority. We don't distinguish well between general ministry and professional ministry. The question remains about what a professional minister can claim as his/her own ground. For example, a focus group of Board members who thought that just about everything was ministry didn't even comprehend the question about where professional ministers derive their authority:

Moderator: By what authority do you think professional clergy do their ministry and make decisions about it in the congregations they serve?

"Ross": I'm not sure I understand.

"John": Me either.

[The question is repeated.]

"John": Oh.

"Samantha": Well.

"Kate": Where does it come from?

Moderator: Yeah.

"Kate": And how was it done?

In an ideal situation, a minister is called to a congregation that has clear governance patterns to guide it. As the minister and the congregation get to know each other and work together they develop a mutual respect. The minister has authority based on a letter of agreement with the congregation, as well as their call. Congregational leaders have the respect of their fellow members, and elected leaders have the support of the congregation. This authority is based on church documents such as bylaws, as well as covenants and formal decisions. Additionally, there is an informal authority based on mutual trust and respect. One focus group participant put it this way:

> But in UUism we have consciously chosen that our congregations are the ultimate authority and so you have that real formal sense that any authority anybody has is something that has been collectively agreed upon by the congregation. And hopefully formalized in your constitution and bylaws. At the same time, there is a very strong informal authority that is given probably to the one person in the congregation that has the least formal authority, and that is the minister."
> —*"Tim," a minister*

Rev. Michael Schuler described it this way in the Service of the Living Tradition at the 2011 General Assembly:

> Whatever respect and credibility a minister enjoys today will, for the most part, reflect the community's estimation of him or her as a *person*. But unlike positional authority, which is automatically conferred, personal authority has to be earned.

The opposite is also true. Informal authority can be withdrawn even faster than it is earned. As a focus group participant said:

> And that's what makes a church different from the workplace. I may not respect my boss and he still has authority, but in the volunteer situation in a church with a minister, if I don't respect the minister, that minister no longer has authority over me.
> —*"John," a Board member*

"And that's what makes a church different from the workplace. I may not respect my boss and he still has authority, but in the volunteer situation in a church with a minister, if I don't respect the minister, that minister no longer has authority over me."
—*"John," a Board member*

In another focus group, one lay leader pointed out that the minister has authority because the congregation wants to be ministered to, and if they don't then the minister no longer has authority. The minister must also minister in the way the congregation wants (such as a social justice emphasis or spiritual emphasis) in order to maintain the relationship.

There is a paradox in defining and tracking authority in a church. There must be clarity about who is responsible for what functions and jobs. However, formal authority must also be flexible so that the informal authority and credibility can flourish. Informal authority cannot be mandated. It flows from the congregation to the minister based on their estimation of the minister as a person. Some focus groups described this as a projection of authority onto the minister. Informal authority is both powerful and fragile.

Lay leaders also have positional and personal authority. Authority flows from the congregation to lay leaders, both those who have formal authority through an elected position and those who hold no position but are ceded authority based on earned respect. Almost every church has a "go-to" person who may or may not hold any formal authority. Those people have a responsibility to use their informal authority in a way that promotes the smooth flow of overall authority within the congregation.

When authority is clear and flexible with respect and trust in place, a church can function smoothly. Disagreements can be resolved without being turned into lingering conflicts. If or when a church and its minister are no longer a good match, possibly because one or the other needs to change, they can part amicably.

However, we know that the situation is not always ideal, and so conflicts develop about ministry and authority. There are many ways to look at these conflicts. The three we use in this report are by situation, by roles and relationships, and by behaviors. Certain situations are more likely than others to generate conflict. Likewise, some types of roles and relationships were mentioned more frequently than others by the people with whom we spoke. From another direction, there are certain behavior patterns that seem to contribute to serious conflict. Some of these are very individual and others seem to be systemic patterns within the denomination. It is also important to note how people with different identities may be affected differently by conflict within the congregation. These factors intertwine and produce a bewildering variety of combinations of real conflicts, as situation, role, and behavior all contribute to making each conflict unique.

Situations

One of the most frequently cited causes of conflict is a change in the size of a congregation, typically when it grows. Many congregations support growth but are not as eager or prepared for the changes that come along with it, such as increasing the number of worship services or having more difficulty parking. Perhaps they are not aware of the changes that generally accompany growth. With growth, the governance pattern often changes, along with the role of the minister. All of this leads to uncertainty about the decision-making processes in the congregation. As one participant pointed out,

> All of a sudden the dynamics are changing, and the governance therefore has to change in your congregation—the way you do things systemically has to change, which creates anxiety and conflict. And then the first thing that sort of gets put on the altar, if you will, is the ministerial authority issue.
> —*"Tim," a minister*

This situation can then lead to congregational conflict, which will often undermine the growth itself as the congregational system seeks to return to a previous way of being. At that time a congregation matriarch or patriarch may play a key role. They may express their support or displeasure either directly through the Board or through open discussion, or they may gather a group of dissenters in the background and question how decisions were made, eventually suggesting that it is the minister's fault that things are going so badly. As a result of this behavior, the minister is likely to be blamed.

In this type of situation and others, sometimes the root cause of the conflict—such as growth and the changes that it necessitates—may be masked by focusing on the trigger of the immediate disagreement. One participant described it this way:

> I've noticed, because of this dynamic, when conflicts do emerge over a decision that has been made, it's very rarely a confrontation with the decision that's been made. It's always the process in which the decision has been made, which is a challenge to the authority in which the decision was made. So, if a group or someone doesn't like a decision that was made, they'll attack the process.
> —*"Tim," a minister*

He went on to say,

> Size transition is a real source of conflict at any stage. The first questions that get asked again are process questions. It's not, "We don't like the fact that our church is growing," which is really the ultimate thing. . . . We don't like the fact that we're losing authority. But the questions are, "Who made this decision?" "How did this decision get made?" And then in that particular size transition

"All of a sudden the dynamics are changing, and the governance therefore has to change in your congregation— the way you do things systemically has to change, which creates anxiety and conflict. And then the first thing that sort of gets put on the altar, if you will, is the ministerial authority issue."
—*"Tim," a minister*

where you don't have the formal structures in place to begin with, there's really room for a lot of criticism as to who's making the decisions and how they're getting done.

—*"Tim," a minister*

The arrival of a new minister is another kind of transition. The formal authority of the minister is defined through the search and call process. A church and its potential new minister enter into a relationship in which the congregation wants the new minister to minister to them and the minister wants to minister to the congregation. They negotiate a formal letter of agreement and establish a covenant. The basic relationship is in place. However, the minister's informal authority is negotiated only through working together.

Authority after a minister has been with a church, in my mind, sort of moves from their credentials—which maybe they have gotten from the UUA and ordination and the training—to now their authority in my mind is defined and reaffirmed by the respect that they receive from the congregation. And that respect is usually shown by attention or even attendance at church.

—*"Samantha," a Board member*

Growth and new ministers are not the only situations that can set the stage for conflict. Staffing changes, a changing neighborhood, or an influx of new members who don't match a congregation's existing demographics can precipitate conflict as the congregational culture shifts and resistance to change emerges, often in the guise of another issue.

A financial crisis in a congregation presents another time of uncertainty and stress. Members will likely put forth many ideas about how to increase revenue or decrease expenses. Individuals of various socioeconomic classes may play out their familial relationships to money in congregational disputes. Naturally, people will disagree on these matters, but there is a danger that old conflicts will resurface in the guise of the current issue or that feelings hurt in the current discussion will become a long-term point of contention between two church factions.

Shifts in theology can also set up a particular kind of conflict. Over the latter half of the last century, Unitarian Universalism moved in a more humanist direction. It is currently moving in a more spiritual direction. The history of the denomination includes other swings in theology. Conflict can arise between differing theological factions, particularly if one had represented the culture of the congregation in the past and another has displaced it. It is often a difficult time for people who feel that their congregation has changed without their agreement. The people who lost out may not address the issue directly, but may instead act out by objecting to every new word and ritual no matter how popular they are with the majority of the congregation. Furthermore, the hurts from these conflicts can linger and resurface for decades.

Situations such as these can create patterns of conflict which linger even after the particular situation has been resolved. One focus group participant talked about a conflict that had happened so many years ago that all thirty to forty people who were involved had died. Yet the memory of the conflict remained alive and thriving and continued to affect current congregational politics. Another noted that during his time as interim minister the congregation took out their frustrations with the previous settled minister on him because they could no longer do it to the previous minister.

Old conflicts that have not been resolved tend to go underground, where they can influence the present. In that form they are not addressed. Previous incidents of clergy misconduct are a particularly difficult issue. The lack of trust and suspicion toward the minister can linger in the church culture for decades, and all subsequent ministers inherit the fallout from one minister's actions.

Roles and Relationships

There are several patterns of roles and relationships that are likely to generate serious conflicts. In focus groups, workshops, and interviews participants smiled in recognition when these were mentioned. Not all churches have conflicts around these issues, but most everyone who participated in the study knew of or had heard of such situations.

For example, the relationship between the minister and the musician was frequently mentioned as particularly subject to conflict. Typically, worship is one of the specific responsibilities of the minister; however, music is a part of the worship service. Musicians are hired to provide music in the church, including worship. Ministers are expert on worship. Musicians are experts on music. They do not always agree on their goals nor do they necessarily agree on who has the greater authority over the music included in the worship service. Tensions in congregations can sometimes result from disagreements over whether and how to incorporate different kinds of music.

This kind of conflict is not limited to worship. In some churches it becomes a conflict between the music program and the church mission as a whole. For instance, one focus group participant described a situation in which the church wanted more rental income, but the music program was using such a high percentage of the facility that there was no room for increased rentals.

As noted in the previous chapter, many congregations have longtime "patriarch" and "matriarch" members who hold a great deal of informal authority—roles which can produce other kinds of conflict. These roles are not inherently bad. But as we saw in the case study earlier in this chapter, they can be a source of conflict for the minister or current lay leadership when they block the flow of authority by insisting that something be done their way. Matriarchs and patriarchs also often have the distinction of being a congregation's biggest donors, which can cause conflict if they attempt to use this fact to wield coercive power. (See "What Is Authority?" page 39.)

Behaviors

Ultimately, it is the way people behave that makes the difference between a resolvable disagreement and a lingering conflict. No particular situation, role, or relationship is the cause of conflict. They are merely the stages on which conflict is played out. Behaviors are the most crucial factors in conflict. Sometimes these are individual bad behavior, such as working from hidden agendas, maintaining poor boundaries, turning individual personality conflicts into all-church struggles, acting disrespectfully, or not staying at the table. The following is an example from one focus group.

> What I heard was there's a group of people who would disagree but they aren't upfront with their disagreement. They're talking in the background and . . . my opinion is you need to short circuit that. They need to be heard but in order for them to be heard, they have to speak up [even] if you have to be in front of the congregation or whatever and say, "Okay, we're going to do this and I know there's a vocal minority who disagree but we want to hear from you and we have to hear it from you."
> —*"Ross," a Board member*

Certain behaviors seem to be common in Unitarian Universalist culture. In a recent essay, Rev. Fredric J. Muir asserts that Unitarian Universalism needs a paradigm shift away from "pervasive, disturbing and disruptive commitment to individualism," "UU exceptionalism that is often insulting to others," and "allergy to authority and power." He believes these are the three organizing and corruptive narratives of our movement. Muir describes well the significance of human behavior as he points to some of the systemic issues that underlie common church conflicts.

Over and over focus group participants talked about our emphasis on the worth of the individual and a background of distrust of authority in Unitarian Universalism. Congregations with a history of not having a minister may see no need for ministerial authority. One lay leader said,

Over and over focus group participants talked about our emphasis on the worth of the individual and a background of distrust of authority in Unitarian Universalism.

First of all, I would say that a minister is not critical to ministry in church. There are those congregations that don't have a minister and everything you described about your congregation was . . . if you didn't have a minister, it would go on. If you had a church administrator but not a minister, I bet your ministry would work really well.

—*"John," a Board member*

Vulnerability in Conflict

Conflicts in congregations have the most negative impact on those who are most vulnerable. As noted in the previous chapter, ministers who more closely approach a cultural standard of a minister are given more power and authority, while those who do not match this standard are given less authority and find their authority more easily revoked (see "Who Has Authority and Who Does Not?," page 53.) We also noted that laypeople with marginalized identities also have a harder time accessing authority in congregations.

Those with marginalized identities—both ministers and lay people—are also more vulnerable to the effects of conflict in congregations. They are less likely to have their voices and perspectives heard and honored, and more likely to be scapegoated. In some situations, such as a dramatic change in the demographics of a congregation, those with marginalized identities can be seen as the problem itself by others in the congregation, but even when this is not true, conflict can have the greatest negative impact on those who are already in precarious positions in our congregations.

Those with marginalized identities, both ministers and lay people, are also more vulnerable to the effects of conflict in congregations. They are less likely to have their voices and perspectives heard and honored, and more likely to be scapegoated.

Implications for Congregational Growth

Many focus group participants mentioned conflicts around authority as contributing to stifling membership growth in congregations. The interruption of a smooth and orderly flow of power and authority, for whatever reason, causes tension and confusion. Newcomers, youth, and people who have traditionally been denied access to power are particularly vulnerable, and their voices are not heard when congregations try to deal with their conflicts. The tension and chaos make it difficult for them to connect to the congregation and to move toward full participation and leadership. They may discover that those who have recently come through a congregational conflict are reluctant to open their circle to newcomers. Thus, newcomers find that their input is not welcome. They may feel the hostility between warring factions. It may be hard to even get a question answered in the

Whatever the specific situation, a congregation filled with uncertainty and conflict is not a comfortable or inspirational place, and newcomers are likely to move on.

chaos. Whatever the specific situation, a congregation filled with uncertainty and conflict is not a comfortable or inspirational place, and newcomers are likely to move on.

Members dedicated to Unitarian Universalism may stay for a short time and try to work out a solution to the struggle. However, those who do not enjoy fighting and are dismayed by the inappropriate behavior around them will eventually leave. When this happens, Unitarian Universalism loses not only members, but also its reputation. Our larger mission to the world is thereby damaged and perhaps even destroyed.

Responding to Conflicts

In this chapter, we do not offer a precise recipe for solving conflicts regarding authority and ministry in our congregations. Instead, we offer a set of responses to the problems we have identified from listening to our participants. In the context of Unitarian Universalism, how can we use our deep faith values to create just, sustainable ministries that encourage trust, authenticity, and liberation? What do we need from our professional ministers and what do they need from each other, our congregations, and the Unitarian Universalist Association to help call such a vision into being?

We have identified ways to shift our attitudes, culture, and institutions that might help us think about, talk about, and engage lovingly and skillfully in conflict. These responses share some common implications:

- From our analysis, we have come to understand authority as the ability to influence and bring about growth and change in an institution, or to block and derail growth and change in an institution.
- We serve on the UUA Commission on Appraisal because we believe in the Unitarian Universalist vision of a beloved community and we believe in congregations which can serve this vision. When asking "Who's In Charge Here?" we have been aware that there are congregational conflicts that undermine this vision. In some ways, this report seeks to interrupt such conflicts and ask: "How did we get here and what is the way out?" We also ask: "What are the spiri-

tual resources we *already have* and how can we direct them toward conflicts of ministry and authority?"

- These conflicts, and our congregations in general, do not operate in a vacuum. As we have reiterated throughout this report, conflicts over ministry and authority are permeated by a cultural context that exposes our communities to particular ways of speaking, listening, and sharing power that lift up or validate particular styles and abilities, and oppress or neglect others.

Establishing Trust

In *Governance and Ministry*, Dan Hotchkiss understands authority as delegated to those who can use their creative powers to interpret and fulfill a piece of a mission, something larger than themselves.[1] Trust is integral to delegating authority to a person or group. Yet we consistently heard from our participants that distrust emerges in conflicts over authority and ministry.

Ministers often speak of pastoral caregiving as a way to establish the trust that is necessary for congregants to give them authority in other ways. Attending to relationships and extending genuine support, compassion, and presence are ways to strengthen the bonds of trust that can de-escalate conflicts and inspire an assumption of good will. This work of building relationships and caring for each other is not confined to professional ministry. Lay members of our congregations can also build trust by attending to each other with compassion and love.

Cultivating Inner Resources

Both ministers and lay leaders need to engage in ongoing work to be responsible agents of the authority they are given.

In addition to tending to relationships, both ministers and lay leaders need to engage in ongoing work to be responsible agents of the authority they are given. For ministers, this includes the ongoing process of discernment, continuing education, self-reflection, and self-care. Critical to this work are effective vehicles for reflection and care, including both individual care such as therapy and spiritual direction, and communities of care, such as groups of supportive colleagues. It is critical that these groups of colleagues offer genuine support of members' full identities, including marginalized identities which don't fit the cultural standard. Lay leaders also have a responsibility to do the work of self-reflection and introspection that allows them to be effective and healthy participants in congregational leadership.

Within the context of ongoing reflection and introspection, ministers and lay leaders can develop the inner resources and skills necessary to become responsible to and for the significant trust represented by leadership in our congregations. Among these skills and resources are the ability to begin with an assumption of good will, the commitment to be clear and honest about one's motivations, the commitment to use respectful communication, the ability to express gratitude for one another's gifts, an ability to come to times of disagreement with an attitude of curiosity, and an ability to differentiate from others in a clear and kind way. Cultivating these will facilitate the building of trust among congregational leaders.

Authorizing Each Other

We suggest that congregational leaders set aside time to struggle together, in order to reach a common understanding about how they are able to authorize each other to do their work. Within these discussions, we might move away from seeing authority and power as limited resources to struggle over. Instead, we might look for the ways in which strong authority given to one person or group in a congregation can strengthen the authority of others. Ministers are more powerful and have more authority when their work is supported, amplified, and grounded by the work of strong lay leadership. Lay leaders are more powerful when ministers have the authority to do the work of ministry, thereby allowing lay leaders to focus on visioning, goal setting, and discernment about mission. We are all more powerful in the world when we see ourselves as on the same team and celebrate each other's strengths.

We suggest that congregational leaders set aside time to struggle together, in order to reach a common understanding about how they are able to authorize each other to do their work.

Balancing Clarity with Flexibility

It is important for both lay and ordained leaders to balance a desire for clarity and transparency with a recognition of the changeable nature of authority in congregations. Many focus group participants longed for clarity in the structures of congregational authority. The Commission was asked over and over to provide a framework that could help answer questions about who should have authority within congregations and who should be responsible for what tasks. We recognize that clarity about these structures and procedures can help liberate congregations. Certainly, we are best served when all people in a congregation—longtime members, newcomers, those who fit the cultural standard, and those who are more marginalized—can discover ways to be heard and to make proposals that will be seriously considered. Congregational systems that rely on simply knowing "the way things are done around here" in order to have access to power are oppressive in many ways. To that end, the Commission wholeheartedly recommends transparency of congregational decision-making systems and structures.

However, we also feel that the quest for clarity can mask the cultural assumption that power and authority are limited, must be carefully apportioned, and may be fixed for all time. In carefully listening to our focus group participants, we discovered that authority does not actually stay within clearly marked lines. Power and authority flow in congregational life. They are constantly being offered and rescinded, sometimes even at the same time by the same people.

Further, the quest to fix structures of authority once and for all limits our congregations in many ways. Systems of authority that work well in one sized congregation do not work well in another size. Systems of authority born out of white dominant culture can block the contributions of those operating out of other cultural frameworks. For an understanding of the idea of systems of authority operating out of other cultural frameworks, we recommend Juana Bordas' *Salsa, Soul, and Spirit*, listed in the list of resources at the end of this book. An overemphasis on clarity can lead to a loss of the life-giving ability to adapt and change.

So, while we recommend that congregations are transparent about their structures, we also recommend against an overemphasis on clarity and encourage a recognition and respect for the changing nature of both congregational membership and systems. We have therefore chosen not to provide a template for the apportionment of authority in congregations. We do, however, respect and recommend the work on congregational systems by authors such as Dan Hotchkiss. In our quest for functioning systems, let us not forget that systems are made up of people, and let us find ways to make the systems of our congregations accessible and responsive.

Taking Advantage of Resources

In moments of deep crisis, congregations can find themselves needing help from outside the congregation. A variety of resources are available to congregational leaders, from UUA publications, including the past reports of this Commission; to the many resources available from the UUA on congregational management. Focus group participants report that such resources are often underutilized, and we hope that congregational leaders will not only use these resources themselves, but also make them known to others in the congregation. See page 89 for a list of recommended resources.

Responding to Theological Differences

As noted earlier, conflicts can emerge not only around the authority for making decisions, but also around the authority for setting the theological

An overemphasis on clarity can lead to a loss of the life-giving ability to adapt and change. So, while we recommend that congregations are transparent about their structures, we also recommend against an overemphasis on clarity and encourage a recognition and respect for the changing nature of both congregational membership and systems.

tone of a congregation, including that of the worship service. These theological conflicts are at odds with our self-understanding as a faith that is open to those with various theological perspectives.

To respond to this, we must remember the covenantal nature of our Unitarian Universalist faith. We are a people bound together by common promises, not common beliefs. Our Unitarian Universalist Principles are a covenant, a set of promises that our congregations have made to each other. We lift up our Principles as a resource to respond to theological conflicts in our congregations.

To respond to theological controversy and create a ground for some of the other work we are suggesting, we envision a revitalization of deep conversation in congregations. We imagine conversations about our Principles, in which members of our congregations ask each other to reflect on what the Principles call us to do in a given situation of tension and conflict. Conversations might include topics such as the meaning of ministry, our wishes and fears about authority and power, our sense of the sacred and the places where we find personal meaning, and the importance of our covenants.

 Similar conversations might engage congregations' own covenants, missions, and visions, reminding them of the foundation of their work together and the larger purposes to which they are dedicated. If these do not exist, or have not been revisited in a while, we suggest deep and intentional conversation to create or renew them.

These conversations might be enriched by some reflection among members of the Unitarian Universalist Ministers Association, to develop a matrix, theology, or language of accountability, trust, faith, and authenticity and by sharing the results of those reflections with our congregations.

Theological controversy is by no means a new phenomenon in Unitarian Universalism. Our congregations do not exist as isolated bodies but are influenced by our own Unitarian, Universalist, and Unitarian Universalist histories and theologies. Belonging to a faith deeply grounded in the context of the United States, our congregations also feel the effects of the shifts in national culture through time. Additionally, the UUA and its member congregations have an institutional history, captured in text and available in oral histories from wise elders in our community who have experienced key institutional events first-hand.

We can share with each other this larger story from several perspectives. There are many UUA curricula and models for teaching our theological histories. These can be used as a tool for resolving conflicts by stepping back to see the larger story and by and focusing on the fundamental causes of the conflict rather than seeing certain people as problematic.

Even more neglected than these resources, though, is our heritage of congregational consultation and admonishment. The Cambridge Platform not only placed covenantal relationships in the center of each congregation,

We must remember the covenantal nature of our Unitarian Universalist faith. We are a people bound together by common promises, not common beliefs. Our Unitarian Universalist Principles are a covenant, a set of promises that our congregations have made to each other.

it also sought to establish covenants between congregations. Our congregations can be resources to each other. Each congregation need not struggle on its own. We are part of a larger whole, and we can help one another to learn the larger story, to see the larger picture, to be drawn back into covenant with each other. Congregation-to-congregation consultation is a rich part of our heritage which should not be neglected.

Responding to Cultural Standards of Leadership

In this report, we have sought to bring the stories of those often at the margins of our associational life into the center of our analysis. We hope that this work will inspire congregations to respond to ongoing structures of privilege and oppression by working to bring to the center the experiences of those at the margins.

Unitarian Universalist communities have been struggling with our relationship to power, privilege, and oppression for quite some time. In this report, we have sought to bring the stories of those often at the margins of our associational life into the center of our analysis. We hope that this work will inspire congregations to respond to ongoing structures of privilege and oppression by working to bring to the center the experiences of those at the margins. This requires us to rethink how power and authority are gained and revoked in congregational systems. Our study participants introduced several potential ways of responding to the issues of conflict over authority and ministry from the margins:

Conduct a power analysis: Two of our interviewees mentioned the importance of conducting a power analysis of a congregation and of the UUA. Mark A. Hicks includes a similar exercise of mapping authority and power in the curriculum *Building the World We Dream About*. Mapping a congregation can show the positions or groups holding power and the various roads to accessing it. In a power analysis, groups can explore the conscious or unconscious stereotypes embedded in the congregation as well as the emotional costs and obstacles for particular individuals and groups. This shows who holds power and how those people or groups make decisions, as well as whether such decisions are made in secret or without collaboration. One interviewee asked, "If leaders are in shared leadership mode, [there may be] confidentiality perhaps, but why would there be secrecy?" A power analysis can help leaders see conflicts over authority in their historical context and part of white dominant culture and shift away from looking at personal intent in these issues. Through understanding how authority is managed in a congregation, leaders can support each other in shifting, as Tema Okun puts it, "to make sense of power, reject fear, [and] embrace love."[2]

Foster relationships in communities of color: It is important to support ministers, religious professionals, and lay leaders of color in fostering relationships in communities of color, both within Unitarian Universalism and outside. Ministers cited their colleagues as one of their sources not just of authority, but also of support in the work of ministry. Ministers and religious professionals of color felt the lack of support from colleagues as a source of stress and difficulty. Strong relationships of support within communities of color are necessary for ministers of color to feel that they have the strong collegial support they need, and congregations need to give their ministers the time and other resources necessary to maintain these relationships.

Engage difference as strength: We agree with "William," a minister in a focus group of religious professionals of color who said, "I think that people of color, people who are marginalized, have something incredibly powerful to give professional ministry within this denomination." If embodied authority is going to be respected, congregations need to be willing to engage difference as a strength in building community, rather than a condition to be shed or overcome. As writer and activist Audre Lorde says, "Difference is that raw and powerful connection from which our personal power is forged."[3]

"I think that people of color, people who are marginalized, have something incredibly powerful to give professional ministry within this denomination."
—"William," a minister

Our work as a Commission with the Developmental Model of Intercultural Sensitivity leads us to believe that there are specific ways congregations can work to build their level of intercultural competence. This work can give congregations tools to develop skills to competently engage difference and find the strengths in diversity. To that end, we recommend "Who Are Our Neighbors?" a recent project of the Unitarian Universalist Ministers Association which provides training in the Developmental Model of Intercultural Sensitivity. This can provide us with the start of a framework to work on developing greater intercultural competence both as a movement and as individuals. We ask congregations to consider engaging in intentional efforts to build greater intercultural awareness and competence.

This work can also support congregations in gaining access to different cultural models which break us out of "either/or" thinking and can help us when "both/and" perspectives are called for. (See "Historical and Cultural Context," page 13.)

Embrace multiple identities: Congregations can teach themselves with curiosity and compassion about the experiences of people who hold multiple marginalized identities, without relying solely on the most marginalized religious professionals to teach them. One religious professional of color remarked that they often try "cutting through that veneer [of 'thin authority'] and going straight for the heart," authentically meeting each person in a congregation where they are.

Institutional Support

Ministers with marginalized identities continue to need ongoing institutional support from the UUA, including visioning, financial resources, and staff support. In addition, programs like the Diversity of Ministry Initiative and Beyond Categorical Thinking, which support congregations in thinking beyond the cultural standard, continue to be necessary. We hope that such programs will continue to be available to Unitarian Universalist ministers and lay leaders. More information about how to access these programs can be found in the list of resources at the end of this book.

The Commission sees this report as the beginning of a conversation, not the end. We hope that we have inspired some reflection about the complexities of ministry and authority in Unitarian Universalist congregations. We hope, too, we have been able to suggest some helpful responses to the complexities of ministry and authority in our congregations. We now entrust this conversation to the broader Unitarian Universalist Association, hopeful that together we can take new steps to realize our aspirations for the beloved community for which we have so long worked and dreamed.

Notes

1. Dan Hotchkiss, *Governance and Ministry: Rethinking Board Leadership* (Herndon, VA: The Alban Institute, 2009), 200.
2. Tema Okun, *The Emperor Has No Clothes: Teaching About Race and Racism to People Who Don't Want to Know* (Charlotte, NC: Information Age Publishing, 2010).
3. Audre Lorde, "The Master's Tools Will Never Dismantle the Master's House," in *Social Theory: The Multicultural and Classic Readings*, ed. Charles Lemert (Boulder, CO: Westview Press, 2009), 450.

Suggested Plan for Discussion

Welcome! Thank you for deciding to plan a congregational discussion in response to this report.

We strongly recommend that you pair this discussion session with the UUA curriculum *Building the World We Dream About*, particularly "Workshop 8: Power at Work in Your Congregation," which develops participants' skills in identifying congregational norms and introduces them to ideas about how power and authority operate in congregational culture.

You might also decide to host a congregation event, in which you have multiple small groups follow the same discussion guide for responding to the report. This guide provides suggestions for conducting such a session. It follows a process similar to the one used by the Commission when using focus groups to create the report, but also allows for some brief initial reflections on the report.

You may also use this format with different questions to explore other topics of interest to your congregation or group of congregations.

Please read through this guide before conducting the session. Also, we recommend that all discussion participants read through the report prior to attending the discussion.

Session Goals

This discussion session will:

- introduce participants to the UUA Commission on Appraisal report *Who's in Charge Here? The Complex Relationship Between Ministry and Authority*
- guide the participants to discern what ministry means in their congregation, who has authority over ministry, and what congregational conflicts and strains are related to ministry and authority
- demonstrate how the congregation members can support each other in responding to conflicts over ministry and authority.

I. Introduction to the Study

This study addresses questions such as:

- Given the unique religious heritage of Unitarian Universalism, our congregational polity, and our diversity, where does ministerial authority within Unitarian Universalist congregations come from?
- What does ministry mean? Why do we call work done by clergy or laity *ministry*?
- From where do lay and ordained ministers draw the authority to minister? What makes someone a minister?
- How are power and authority in ministry shared or distributed in our congregations?
- How can we comprehend a source of authority which is grounded in our covenantal faith and which leads us towards health and growth?

In writing this report, the Commission listened to focus group participants for stories that allow us to go deeper. This discussion guide is an invitation to deep listening and respectful sharing. We recommend that you prepare a set of ground rules or covenant that encourages safe and responsible participation by all members in the session. You may want to use a covenanting process provided in UUA curricula such as *The Safe Congregation Handbook* or *Building the World We Dream About*.

II. Composition and Recruitment of Discussion Group: Some Options

Groups should have 6–12 participants. You may decide that this discussion is open to all and bring together a multi-generational sample of people in the congregation from diverse roles. Alternatively, you may choose to bring together a group of people who hold similar roles in the congregation (such as a group of staff, the Membership Committee, or the Board). It is best if a leader with pastoral ministry skills serves as a chaplain.

Call or email potential participants to invite them to the meeting. Send them a follow-up invitation with an agenda. About three days before the session, call each member to remind them to attend. Participants should be told that the group discussion will last 1.5–2 hours. If your discussion group is part of a larger event, such as a Board meeting, there may be an additional group report-out time. This session may help guide future discussions and tasks for the congregation.

In addition to recruiting participants, we strongly recommend that you recruit a moderator and note-taker for your discussion. The moderator will facilitate the discussion and encourage the full, relaxed participation of all participants. We also want the conversation to allow new conversations to emerge that we did not think to ask about. The note-taker will document the perspectives shared in the dialogue. You should decide whether they will leave voices anonymous in the notes, or if they will ask individuals' permission to record their names.

III. Set-Up

Hold the discussion in a location where participants can sit comfortably and see each other easily. Have writing implements and paper on hand for each participant.

Materials List

You will need the following materials for your focus group

- a copy of the Commission's report
- water and cups for all participants, moderator, and note-taker
- discussion outline for all participants
- writing paper or index cards for all participants
- pens and/or pencils for all participants

IV: Session Guide

A. Introduction

- Greet participants as they arrive and invite them to wear nametags. Give each participant a writing implement and some paper.
- Gather the group with a short reading and/or chalice lighting.
- Introduce yourself and the Commission's study, unless your group is part of a larger event where this has already been done.
- Introduce the note-taker and let the participants know that the notes will be taken. If you have decided to document names as well as perspectives, remind participants of this.
- Provide a covenant to ground the discussion or engage in a covenanting activity to develop a group covenant for the session.

B. Leading the Discussion

You will be asking participants a list of questions. For each question, give them a minute or so to write notes to themselves, if they wish. Let participants know that these notes are only for themselves and will not be collected. This gives people a chance to get their own thoughts together, and helps to undermine "group think," or the quelling of disagreement.

C. Managing the Conversation

It is important to make sure that each participant answers the first and last questions listed in section D, which serve as an icebreaker and a check-out question, respectively. For the other questions, the conversation can be a bit more fluid. If participants want to respond to each other and build off each other, that is great. Notice the dynamics. Is there someone who hasn't spoken? Invite them gently to speak if you think it is appropriate. Is someone dominating the conversation? Gently suggest that the group might want to hear from those who haven't spoken yet. Listen for the development of "group think." If there is a minority position that is struggling to be heard, offer support as appropriate.

When you feel that it is losing momentum or has stopped being relevant, bring the group back to the original question. You can do this by restating the question, or perhaps by calling on someone who hasn't spoken and asking for their thoughts while restating the question.

Closure on each question means that everyone has spoken who has something to contribute and the conversation feels complete. It does not necessarily mean everyone in the group agrees. Expect different points of view in the group; disagreement is fine.

You should keep track of time or appoint someone to make reminders about the time remaining for each question.

If the group is very talkative, you may need to create closure on each question in order to have time for all the questions. You might say, "We have only a few more minutes to discuss this question. Is there anything pressing that hasn't been said yet?" You can also remind participants of the number of questions remaining and the time remaining to help with time management. If the group is less talkative, you may need to ask follow-up questions. Do not force the group to keep talking about a question that just doesn't interest them. But if you think they are just being shy, you could ask participants to expand on what they've said.

Let the conversation on the last question run for as long as it has energy or until the end of the announced time. Make sure to end the group on time.

D. Questions

Introduction: I have several questions to ask you. First comes a set of fact questions to help you introduce yourself to the rest of us. For these, let's go around the circle to answer. The answers need to be very brief—just a sentence or two, no whole paragraphs. I will go first to show you what I have in mind.

1. What is your name? What drew you to this congregation?

Further instruction: I have brought along some pens (or pencils) and some paper (or index cards) in case you don't have them with you. For the next several questions, I invite you to take a few moments after I read each question to reflect on it silently and then to jot down a few notes. I will read each question twice. After everyone has had time to write some notes, I will let you know when I'm ready to hear your answers. I invite you to speak in whatever order you choose.

2. I would like to gather some of your initial thoughts by asking you to reflect briefly on two items, based on your reading of the COA report:
  * *something new you learned*
  * *a question that the report brought up for you.*

3. We call some things, but not all things, that happen in congregations ministry. *What goes on in your congregation that you would call ministry? Who does these things? What goes on in the congregation that you consider not to be part of the ministry?*

Further instruction: Next come two related questions. We will take them up one at a time. After I read the first one twice, I will give you time to reflect and write on it and then share your answers with the rest of us. When we have finished with that question, I will read the second one.

4a. Turn your attention to professional clergy who minister to your congregation. Where do you think they get the authority to do their ministry and to make decisions about how they will do it?

4b. Now turn your attention to the laypeople in the congregation. What gives them the authority to make decisions that affect ministry in their congregations, especially the ministry carried out by professional clergy?

Further instruction: Next come two more related questions. Again, we will take them up one at a time. After I read the first one twice, I will give you time to reflect and write on it and then share your answers with the rest of us. When we have finished with that question, I will read the second one.

5a. In your experience, to what extent do differences of opinion about ministry and authority contribute to congregational stresses and strains?

5b. What ideas do you have about how to overcome stresses and strains due to differences of opinion about ministry and authority?

Further instruction: We are now ready for the final question. For this one, after you have time for reflection and writing, I am going to ask that you go around the circle so that I hear from everyone in sequence.

6. What else would you like your congregation to investigate and think about regarding the relationship between ministry and authority?

At the end of your conversation, please let your participants know that the Commission on Appraisal is always happy to receive comments and feedback about current studies, as well as ideas for future studies.

V. After the Group

As the group ends, please thank the participants for attending and helping in the discussion.

After the group ends, you should sit down and write up a report of the experience. How did the group go? What patterns and themes emerged in the answers to the questions? What went well? What was difficult or problematic? What were your overall impressions?

Next, decide as a group what action items came out of the discussion. For example, the group might have discovered that its understanding of who is responsible for parts of ministry in the congregation differ from those job or volunteer descriptions. Or the conversation might have addressed parts of the congregation's governance structure, and congregational leadership might benefit from further discussion of these reflections. You might create a chart that lists the "Action," "Purpose," "Resources," and "Responsible Party," so that the results of the discussion do not get lost.

You might decide to have the note-taker create a transcript of the conversation. If you decide to do this, be sure to follow your agreement about whether to document participants' names or to leave perspectives and comments anonymous.

You may decide that particular leaders or groups within the congregation should have a similar discussion of their own, or read the results of this discussion group as well as the action items the planners developed after the session ended.

If your conversation yields ideas that you would like to share with the Commission on Appraisal, please contact the Commission by email: coa@uua.org. Stay connected to the COA by visiting our website: www.uua.org/coa.

Resources

Unitarian Universalist Resources

Beyond Categorical Thinking Program

The Beyond Categorical Thinking (BCT) program works with Unitarian Universalist congregations to promote inclusive thinking and help prevent unfair discrimination in the ministerial search process. Congregations can access the program through the UUA Transitions Office: transitions@uua.org.

Diversity of Ministry Initiative

The Diversity of Ministry Initiative (DOMI) seeks to foster, create, and sustain healthy, engaged, long-term ministries for ministers and religious professionals who identify as people of color, Latina/o, Hispanic, and/or multiracial/multiethnic. More information can be found at: www.uua.org/multiculturalism/dom/index.shtml.

Building the World We Dream About Curriculum

Building the World We Dream About is a Unitarian Universalist program that seeks to interrupt the workings of racism and transform how people from different racial/ethnic groups understand and relate to one another. It consists of 24 two-hour workshops, with Taking It Home activities, reflections, and readings to be done between workshops. The program can be found at: www.uua.org/re/tapestry/adults/btwwda/index.shtml.

Congregational Management Resources

There are many helpful resources gathered in one place to help congregational leaders: www.uua.org/management/index.shtml.

Searching for the Future Weekend Workshops from the Congregational Stewardship Consulting Program

The Commission encourages our congregations to participate in intentional conversations about their missions and visions. The "Searching for the Future" weekend, offered by the UUA's Congregational Stewardship Consulting Program, is an excellent facilitated program designed to help congregations have this conversation. We recommend that congregations who do not have explicit mission and vision statements, or who have not revisited their mission and vision statements in the last five years, consider planning one of these weekends with the help of the Stewardship Consulting office.

Who Are Our Neighbors? Program of the Unitarian Universalist Ministers Association

"Who Are Our Neighbors?" is a program to explore multiculturalism and develop our intercultural competencies within the UUMA. Thirty UUMA facilitators have been trained by Beth Zemsky and Phyllis Braxton from One Ummah Consulting, and will be leading trainings in chapters and regional gatherings around the continent through the spring of 2014. UUMA members can access the program through their chapters. See www.uuma.org/?whoareneighbors for more information.

Other Resources

The Center for Non-Violent Communication

The attitude with which we approach any conversation can have a direct impact on the flow of authority in our congregations. The Commission recommends that congregations explore non-violent communication training for leaders and other lay members as a part of the leadership development process.

The Center for Non-Violent Communication says this about its training: "With NVC we learn to hear our own deeper needs and those of others. Through its emphasis on deep listening—to ourselves as well as others—NVC helps us discover the depth of our own compassion. This language reveals the awareness that all human beings are only trying to honor universal values and needs, every minute, every day." See their website: www.cnvc.org.

One Ummah Consulting

One Ummah is a team of consultants and trainers who have come together from a broad range of fields to assist organizations in building their multicultural competence. One Ummah Consultants have helped both the UU Ministers Association and the Commission on Appraisal with work on diversity, inclusion, and intercultural competence. See their website: www.oneummahconsulting.com.

Books

Adams, James Luther. "The Prophethood of All Believers" in *The Essential James Luther Adams*. Ed. George Kimmich Beach. Boston: Skinner House, 1998.

This essay is an argument for prophethood in general, for the role of the liberal church in proclaiming social justice values. Adams insists that the role of prophet belongs to everyone. Interestingly, it seems unclear whether he means everyone individually or whether he envisions prophethood as an entirely collective endeavor. Here is the key paragraph:

> We have long held to the idea of the *priesthood* of all believers, the idea that all believers have direct access to the ultimate resources of the religious life and that every believer has the responsibility of achieving an explicit faith for free persons. As an element of the radical laicism we need also a firm belief in the *prophethood* of all believers. The prophetic liberal church is not a church in which the prophetic function is assigned merely to the few. The prophetic liberal church is the church in which persons think and work together to interpret the signs of the times in the light of their faith, to make explicit through discussion the epochal thinking that the times demand. The prophetic liberal church is the church in which all members share the common responsibility to attempt to foresee the consequences of human behavior (both individual and institutional), with the intention of making history in place of merely being pushed around by it. Only through the prophetism of all believers can we together foresee doom and mend our common ways.

Adams, James Luther. "Radical Laicism" in *The Prophethood of All Believers*. Ed. George K. Beach. Boston: Beacon Press, 1986.

In this essay, Adams argues that the laity has a vocation: "[A] hand, an imperative hand, is laid upon us, giving us a religious vocation." He believes that the laity on whom this hand is laid includes not just members of congregations, but also non-religious people and ordained ministers, whom he says are also a part of the laity—the "people."

Taken together, his descriptions of the priesthood and prophethood of the laity basically define ministry for him. These are both roles to which all people are called, and particularly regarding the transformation of the church, he recognizes that this is sometimes best done from outside. There is a tension between the individual and the collective vocation. He is more explicit in this essay: "Radical laicism . . . has asserted that the creative and transforming powers are accessible to the individual but at the same time call for the covenant of common responsibilities."

Arnason, Wayne, and Kathleen Rolenz. *Worship That Works: Theory and Practice for Unitarian Universalists*. Boston: Skinner House, 2008.

This book is an excellent example of case study research regarding worship.

Bordas, Juana. *Salsa, Soul, and Spirit: Leadership for a Multicultural Age*. San Francisco: Berrett-Koehler Publishers, 2007.

This book addresses the character of leadership but does not discuss the structure of leadership much. The author describes a leadership model with characteristics based on the best leadership from Latino, African American, and Native American traditions and cultures. The message is an important one for this age of greed and individualism. The characteristics Bordas describes are what we would hope to see in all leaders. While written in a way that seems to be as much hype as fact, this book reminds us that there are different cultural models of leadership that need to be considered when analyzing and recommending models of authority in our congregations.

Child, Barbara. *The Shared Ministry Sourcebook*. Boston: UUA, 1996.

As we note in our report, the term *shared ministry* has become a bit of a buzz phrase and so has lost some of its meaning. This book helped us in our understanding of the vision of shared ministry as a project within Unitarian Universalism when it still meant something powerful and specific. The book addresses the character of shared ministry and gives numerous examples of shared ministry programs at work in Unitarian Universalist congregations.

Commission on Appraisal. *Interdependence: Renewing Congregational Polity*. Boston: Skinner House, 1997.

This report of the Commission touches on our current study in three ways. First, it recognizes the duality of power in a congregation. The minister is *called* by the congregation, and the Board is *elected* by the congregation. If a church is to thrive (or even survive well), this dual power must be recognized and must find ways to "foster mutual accountability among clergy, lay leadership, and membership for the advancement of the Mission-Covenant."

Second, it raises the importance of shared ministry. Barbara Child serves as a key resource in the section on shared ministry. The report makes the important point that "volunteers are not subject to adequate screening, training, and supervision while they are involved in lay ministry."

Finally, this report maintains that some hierarchy is necessary for effective governance. Tom Chulak says,

> Without some hierarchy it is my experience that groups become stagnant, orthodox, and rigid. They become oppressive. Why? Because what happens in human community when you do not delegate authority to certain roles and Boards is those who have the greatest need for control and power will move into the center and there will be no way to move these persons out and eventually the group will die. Those groups which do not pay attention to structure—to roles and relationships and the need to have leadership—become the most anti-Unitarian Universalist.

Friedman, Edwin H. *Generation to Generation: Family Process in Church and Synagogue*. New York: Guilford Press, 1985.

Friedman's basic thesis is presented in chapter nine, "Leadership and Self." He writes: "It will be the thesis of this chapter that the overall health and functioning of any organization depends primarily on one or two people at the top, and that this is true whether the relationship system is a personal family, a sports team, an orchestra, a congregation, a religious hierarchy, or an entire nation. But the reason for that connection is not some mechanistic, trickle-down, domino effect. It is, rather, that leadership in families, like leadership in any flock, swarm, or herd is essentially an organic, perhaps even biological, phenomenon. And an organism tends to function best when its "head" is well differentiated. The key to successful spiritual leadership, therefore, with success understood not only as moving people toward a goal, but also in terms of the survival of the family (and its leader) has more to do with the leader's capacity for self-definition than with the ability to motivate others."

Friedman asserts that leaders need to be able to differentiate, while still remaining engaged with their followers (the congregation.) He directs us to look at the congregation or its subgroups (Board, staff, choir) as a system. When conflict arises, we look at the entire system, and especially the relationship of the leader to other members of the group. It is also critical for the leader to examine their relationship to both the leader's family of origin and current family structure. Patterns of behavior often carry over from families to congregations. Friedman's work is foundational in the understanding of systemic patterns of authority in congregations.

Hill, Robert L. *The Complete Guide to Small Group Ministry: Saving the World Ten at a Time*. Boston: Skinner House, 2003.

This is mostly a book of directions for congregations beginning small group ministry programs. Hill mentions several authority issues that can arise when congregations institute small group ministry. In some congregations, the minister is in charge of the program: choosing and training facilitators, choosing topics and resources for the group sessions, and assigning people to groups. This is sometimes more authority than a congregation is used to granting the minister.

On the other hand, facilitators have a great deal of authority in any small group ministry program, especially for the participants in their own group. A small group ministry program can cause a shift away from the minister as lone ranger model to a model of shared ministry. Hill notes, "John Morgan, writing for *Covenant Group News* in March 2000 says, 'Small group Ministry will change the very nature of our churches and the leadership which guides them. One minister simply cannot be "in charge" of a church which adopts a small group ministry. It takes a different model of ministry—shared ministry—to work.'" Hill mentions ministers who were surprised by the aspects of their role that naturally fell to facilitators or small groups as a whole when a small group ministry program had been instituted.

Hotchkiss, Dan. *Governance and Ministry: Rethinking Board Leadership*. Herndon, VA: Alban Institute, 2009.

Hotchkiss lays out a recommended structure for facilitating effective ministry in congregations. In this structure, the Board as chief governing body needs to choose wisely which few subjects merit congregational attention and then foster rich dialogue about them. The Board should have few committees to help the Board do its policy work. The Board's job is making policy, not deciding cases.

In this structure, the minister serves as head-of-staff model, with the expectation of consultation. The minister directs the work of ministry through teams rather than committees, such as: worship, religious education, social action, hospitality, caring, choir, stewardship, newsletter, and garden. (Hotchkiss distinguishes between teams and committees by saying that the product of a committee is words on paper; the product of a ministry team is action.)

Using this model, the congregation does the discernment work about mission, and is the main labor pool for ministry. The most successful congregations are those that focus on mission rather than organization for its own sake.

Hotchkiss also has lots to say about the pitfalls of other types of structures in congregations, specifically the stresses and strains they create in the apportioning and exercise of authority.

Mathews, Rosita deAnn. "Using Power from the Periphery," in *A Troubling in My Soul: Womanist Perspectives on Evil and Suffering*. Ed. Emilie Townes. Maryknoll, NY: Orbis Books, 1993.

We drew our definition of power from the periphery from this work.

McKeeman, Gordon. "Theology of Power in the Ministry," in *Unitarian Universalism: Selected Essays*. Boston: The Unitarian Universalist Ministers Association, 2001.

In this essay, McKeeman defines ministry as "participating in a leadership role in which people are invited to become mature religious persons," and defines eight steps in cultivating spiritual maturity. McKeeman also identifies and discusses three sources of the power to do ministry: knowledge, personal spiritual practice, and reverence.

Muir, Fredric J. "The End of the iChurch," in *Assembled 2012: Select Sermons and Lectures from the General Assembly of the Unitarian Universalist Association*. Boston: Skinner House, 2012.

Muir asserts that Unitarian Universalism needs a paradigm shift away from: pervasive and disruptive commitment to individualism, UU exceptionalism that insults others, and allergy to authority and power. He calls these the three organizing and corruptive narratives of our movement. The old way he calls the iChurch. The new way he calls the beloved community. His "i" stands for individualism (as inherited from Emerson), and he believes that we cannot do individualism and covenant at the same time. The second and third problems are seen as an outgrowth of individualism. He says that the aversion to authority makes it difficult to welcome different opinions and passions.

Sawyer, Ken. "It's the Minister: The Mystery and Wonder of the Role," Berry Street Essay, delivered in Portland, OR, June 20, 2007. www.uuma. org/Page/BSE2007.

Sawyer writes about the mysterious way that people give ministers a special place, based on the role they expect them to play. And often ministers respond by growing into that role—even if it is not their natural mode of being. "The truth is, it is difficult to succeed in ministry if in your spoken world you are silent, snooty, and snide. Inauthentic as it may well be at times, polite, cheerful, and tolerant are what the role calls for, and fairly," he says.

Schuler, Michael. "The Face of God or a Face in the Crowd?" Sermon given at the General Assembly Service of the Living Tradition. Charlotte, North Carolina. June 23, 2011, www.uua.org/ga/past.

Schuler addresses anti-authoritarianism which he says is a long-standing aspect of American character. He notes that respect for and influence of clergy has waxed and waned over the centuries, but is at a low point now. Ministers' self-esteem is also declining. He defines authority as power freely conferred in consideration of services rendered. It has both positional and personal components. The personal authority must be earned through love, trust, authenticity, and partnership. The positional clout is less than it used to be. He quotes John Buehrens: "Don't try to use any authority until they give it to you, for in the end it is conferred by trust and that must be earned." Ministers also have to be secure enough to share the church's ministry. Schuler says that we must come to terms with the authority issues which plague our churches and keep them in chaos.

Schwendeman, Jill M. *When Youth Lead: A Guide to Intergenerational Social Justice Ministry*. Boston: UUA, 2007.

This is mostly a handbook for those doing youth ministry, and thus much of it is not relevant to our study. However, it includes a few important points, including an interesting definition of ministry:

> Although people often think of ministry as the work of an ordained minister, in a congregation that embraces the unique contributions of every person, youth can play a vibrant ministerial role. . . . In every congregation, there are . . . myriad quiet ministries. . . . Each person, from the youngest baby to the quietest adult, can be a minister to those around them in ways that may not be obvious but are still important to the life of the congregation. In this broad sense, "ministry" refers to our interactions with one another that enrich, comfort, and challenge our spiritual selves.

The author lists "pressure on the church door" (challenging us to be inclusive), playfulness, sharing individual skills, and validating the children as the ministries of teens.

One of the themes of the book is shared power. Schwendeman offers a model of youth ministry that combines youth empowerment and decision-making with adult guidance in partnership. She sees youth ministry as ideally being ministry *to* and *with* youth—offering something to youth, but also honoring the ministry youth have to offer.

Sewell, Marilyn. "Power," in *The Growing Church: Keys to Congregational Vitality*. Ed. Thom Belote. Boston: Skinner House, 2010.

This article contains some important insights about authority in Unitarian Universalist congregations, including an emphasis on the importance of ensuring that authority and accountability are given in tandem. Sewell also stresses the importance of ministers and lay leaders claiming and owning the power they do have, in order to be effective and accountable.

Stevens, Paul R. and Phil Collins. *The Equipping Pastor: A Systems Approach to Congregational Leadership*. Washington, DC: Alban Institute, 1993.

An excerpt sums up the thesis of this book well: "The church is stuck. The reason for the unreleased congregational potential is much deeper than the problem of clericalism of pastors protecting their turf. We are convinced that the stagnation of the laity is caused mainly by the frustrating power of a church system that keeps the laity marginalized and prevents the pastor from doing the most important work: 'equipping the laity for the work of the ministry.' . . . The equipping pastor is not merely one who gets the lay people to assist her or him. No, the equipping pastor assists the people to fulfill their own ministry, a much greater thing."

The book goes on to outline a variety of leadership styles and their impact on a congregation from a systems perspective. It also provides an analysis of how to effectively use a variety of leadership styles to equip the lay members of a congregation to do effective ministry.

Taylor, Douglas. "Mother, Moses, or a Spiritual ATM? Archetypes of Authority in Contemporary Liberal Religion," in *Unitarian Universalism: Selected Essays*. Boston: The Unitarian Universalist Ministers Association, 2002.

Taylor discusses expectations of a minister in terms of archetypes as a source of authority. He discusses some common archetypes for ministerial authority, and the situations in which they are most effective. He claims that all ministers have a predisposition to one or more of these archetypes, and he urges ministers to know their archetype and "lean into it." He also discusses the role of projection in the work of exercising ministerial authority.

Wesley, Alice Blair. *Our Covenant, The 2000–2001 Minns Lectures*. Chicago: Meadville Lombard Theological School Press, 2002.

Wesley emphasizes the history and implications of the covenantal free church, that is, congregational organization. She defines a covenantal free church as "a body of individuals who have freely made a profoundly simple promise, a covenant: We pledge to walk together in the spirit of mutual love. The spirit of love alone is worthy of our ultimate, our religious loyalty. So we shall meet often to take counsel concerning the ways of love, and we will yield religious authority solely to our own understanding of what these ways are, as best we can figure them or learn or remember them together." As she sees it, authentic authority comes only from the members of each free church, and that authority is expressed through their covenant. She believes that patterns of empowerment exist and must be visible if they are going to function well.

Methodology Resources

We consulted the following works in designing the methodology for this study.

Krueger, Richard A. *Focus Groups: A Practical Guide for Applied Research.* Newbury Park: Sage Publications, 1988.

Lofland, John, and Lyn H. Lofland. *Analyzing Social Settings: A Guide to Qualitative Observation and Analysis.* Belmont: Wadsworth Publishing Company, 1995.

Maykut, Pamela, and Richard Morehouse. *Beginning Qualitative Research: A Philosophic and Practical Guide.* New York: RoutledgeFalmer, 1994.

Morgan, David. *Focus Groups as Qualitative Research.* Second Edition. Thousand Oaks, CA: Sage Publications, 1997.

Neuman, W. Lawrence. *Social Research Methods: Qualitative and Quantitative Approaches.* Fifth Edition. Boston: Allyn and Bacon, 2003.

Platt, Jennifer. "Cases of Cases . . . of Cases," in *What Is a Case?* Eds. Charles C. Ragin and Howard S. Becker. Cambridge: Cambridge University Press, 1992.

West, Traci C. *Disruptive Christian Ethics: When Racism and Women's Lives Matter.* Louisville: Westminster John Knox Press, 2006.